FIRST-TIME DAD'S JOURNEY TO PARENTHOOD

ULTIMATE GUIDE TO MASTER THE ART OF NEWBORN CARE, SAY GOODBYE TO PARENTING JITTERS, GET HANDS-ON WITH YOUR NEWBORN, & TRANSITION SMOOTHLY FROM HUSBAND TO HERO

DADDY BOOT CAMP

CONTENTS

INTRODUCTION

> *The nature of fatherhood is that you're doing something that you're unqualified to do, and then you become qualified when you do it.*

JOHN GREEN

It's your first night alone with your precious newborn. You cradle them, feeling overwhelmed and uncertain. You want to be the best dad possible, but questions fill your mind. How do you change a diaper without any mishaps? Is the baby's crying normal, and how can you soothe them? The responsibilities and expectations of fatherhood can be daunting.

That's where *Daddy Boot Camp* comes in. We understand the challenges and anxieties of being a first-time father, and we're here to guide you every step of the way. No more second-guessing or feeling lost; it's time to embrace your role with confidence.

Get ready for a journey filled with valuable lessons. First, we'll boost your confidence, helping you leave behind those nagging doubts. You'll tackle parenting tasks with certainty, having mastered diaper changes, feedings, and baby care. Next, we'll focus on effective bonding – the secret to building an unbreakable connection with your little one. Feeling stressed? Learn to stay calm under the pressures of fatherhood and discover self-care strategies.

But that's not all. Teamwork is key! Learn how to maintain harmony at home while sharing parenting duties. You're not just a dad; you're a supportive partner. Dive into your role during pregnancy, birth, and early parenthood, charging through the journey like a stampede of encouragement and strength. We'll guide you through understanding the physical and emotional changes that come with this journey. Maintaining a strong relationship amidst the chaos? We've got your back. Plus, we'll emphasize the importance of self-care for both parents.

Parenting comes with its challenges and concerns. Let's tackle some super-dad training: mastering diaper changes and baby care – sans capes, but loaded with superhero vibes! Then, face the infamous sleep deprivation with our tricks to help you through those sleepless nights. Don't forget the daily juggling act of balancing work, family, and maintaining your cool-dad status. Adaptability is key, as life is about to change in many ways. Don't neglect self-care amidst the diaper changes and baby giggles—even heroes need a break.

Feeling the pressure to be the ultimate dad? Relax; you've got this, and we're here to guide you. Uncertainty and insecurity may linger, but we'll give you some tools to help overcome those fears. Just remember that no one is fully prepared for large life changes and no one is perfect; however, you can have tools in the back pocket to help through those difficult times that will try you as a man. We hope this book helps to give you some idea of what to expect and how you can navigate the road ahead.

John Green's quote powerfully captures the transformative nature of fatherhood. It's a path that starts with self-doubt and feeling unqualified, but through experiences and love, fathers grow into their roles, becoming highly competent and loving parents over time. No one is born knowing all the answers, but through the journey of parenting, fathers become qualified and loving dads, one step at a time. Embrace the journey, cherish every moment, and know that you are becoming an exceptional dad.

CHAPTER 1
THE FIRST-TIME DADDY JOURNEY BEGINS

Any fool can have a child. That doesn't make you a father. It's the courage to raise a child that makes you a father.

BARACK OBAMA

It all begins with a life-altering realization, that moment of pure wonder when you discover you're going to be a dad. This feeling is thrilling, slightly nerve-wracking, and filled with the promise of an unforgettable adventure.

Today's dads are not the same as the dads of the past. You're not merely a provider; you're an active and nurturing part of your child's life. This is a new era of dadhood, brimming with opportunities to make a positive impact on your child's development, happiness, and future achievements.

Engaged fathers like yourself significantly contribute to their children's well-being and lay the essential foundation for a strong and loving bond. From heartwarming interactions to guidance, your role as a dad is nothing short of indispensable.

However, being a great dad doesn't just happen by chance. It begins with intention. We will not only highlight the right steps to take but also point out some common mistakes to avoid. This way, you can approach fatherhood with mindfulness, understanding, and the unwavering determination to build a beautiful and lasting relationship with your child.

THE MEANINGFUL JOURNEY OF FATHERHOOD: REALIZING ITS SIGNIFICANCE

As with all big life changes, discovering you're going to be a father is a whirlwind of emotions, from pure joy to moments of shock, and fear, and back to overwhelming joy. The uncertainty of the unknown makes it challenging to process. Stepping into this chapter, it's normal to be filled with a sense of expectation and responsibility that keeps you up at night. The journey to fatherhood is incredible, but can also be daunting, especially since resources for expectant dads are not as abundant as those for expectant moms. It's no wonder that many soon-to-be dads grapple with anxiety (Allen, 2022).

Emotionally, you might feel unprepared. Questions about your relationship with the mother, your connections with others in your life, and your family dynamics may arise. Becoming a father often leads to reflecting on our relationships with our fathers and contemplating the type of parent we want to be (Becoming Dad—A Guide for New Fathers, 2021). If you're like us, you live a very different life than your parents and have different expectations in life. As we were approaching parenthood, many of our thoughts and talks centered around how we fit a little one into those expectations – how we maintain a life where we are getting the most out of it, providing everything for our baby, and still maintaining our sanity in the process.

It can be a tough balancing act, managing your expectations, your loved one's goals, the process of pregnancy, and raising a little one; however, please know you're not alone! Having these thoughts and just the process of considering the parent you want to be, the goals you want to pursue as a team with your partner, and allowing yourself to embrace these emotions are the unique parts of becoming a father. Be open, communicate, recognize what you're feeling, and don't feel shy to bring others into the conversation.

Becoming a Father: A Journey That Begins Before Birth

Becoming a dad starts with that unforgettable instant when you and your partner discover you're having a baby. This stirs up a mix of emotions, from excitement and happiness to moments of uncertainty and doubt.

During pregnancy you're not just an observer; you actively participate. You'll accompany your partner to prenatal appointments, ultrasounds, and check-ups. Your role goes beyond providing emotional support; you'll take on new responsibilities like managing household chores, cooking meals, and ensuring your partner's comfort during pregnancy.

And it's worth it! Just wait until you see that first ultrasound of your baby – it's utterly life-changing and feel almost awestruck.

As an expectant dad, you dive into learning about pregnancy, childbirth, and parenting. You may read books, attend parenting classes, or seek advice from experienced parents. This knowledge allows you to connect the dots between the physical and emotional changes your partner experiences and the journey of fetal development.

We found that engaging our friends with children helped. They've been there, ran the gauntlet, and have the insight that may help you build out your roadmap.

But this journey isn't just a mental one; it's also intensely emotional! It's essential to have open conversations with your partner about these feelings and seek support from friends, family, or professionals if needed. Talking through how you're feeling and any doubts you may have can help manage those emotions. Keeping them in only adds to the anxiety! So, while as guys, we send one-word texts and avoid long phone calls at any cost, talking through this can be very beneficial. Have a guy's night, grab some beers, and talk through it – your buddies are there for you.

As the due date approaches, you start to prepare. You gather stories and experiences from those who've been through this journey before. You may even connect with other expectant fathers, building a camaraderie founded on shared anticipation and a shared desire to be the best fathers you can be. Together with your partner, you plan how you'll share responsibilities and care for your little one.

The plan is everything and can reduce tensions in the future with your partner. It's almost like hedging your risk in Fantasy Football with that handcuff pick – plan for the future.

We found that establishing responsibilities up front or at least discussing them made for a smoother process once we were in the daily grind of caring for our little one. We developed a timetable of caring for when we could either rest or take on baby care, allowing each of us to get time with the baby and also to rest and relax.

This journey isn't straightforward; it's an adventure filled with emotions, education, and preparation. It's about stepping into fatherhood with excitement, uncertainty, and love.

SHAPING FUTURES: THE DISTINCT ROLES OF DADS IN THEIR CHILD'S LIFE

Today's fatherhood is far removed from the distant and detached roles of fathers in the past; now sexy, hands-on dads are an integral part of raising their children. Modern fathers are actively engaged in their children's lives, and research has highlighted the positive impact they bring. Studies show that children with engaged fathers experience enhanced cognitive and language development, improved social skills, and an increased likelihood of academic success (Embracing Modern Fatherhood, n.d.).

The importance of fathers in their children's lives extends beyond immediate family dynamics. Having both a mother and father figure is essential for a child's holistic development.

Those who had actively involved father figures during child-hood tend to have stronger, enduring marriages and often become involved parents themselves in the future (Embracing Modern Fatherhood, n.d.). As fathers take on more active roles in childcare, it can reduce stress levels for mothers, leading to a healthier and more balanced home life for everyone.

Furthermore, fathers' interactions, guidance, and nurturing play a significant role in shaping a child's future. They contribute to forming a unique, yet equally powerful bond compared to the mother-child relationship (Machin, 2021). Both mothers and fathers foster these bonds, but fathers intro-duce an essential element of challenge. This challenge reflects their role in supporting their child's growth beyond the family unit.

Across a diverse tapestry of cultures, fathers universally earn their stripes as trailblazers of child development, fearlessly acquainting their offspring with the thrill of risk and the art of embracing challenges. These experiences help children develop the resilience required to thrive in our demanding world. One of the most effective ways fathers achieve this is through play. Play provides children with opportunities to explore their limits, discover their capabilities, and learn how to navigate challenges, all under the guidance and encouragement of their fathers.

CHARTING YOUR PARENTING PATH: SETTING INTENTIONS FOR A UNIQUE JOURNEY

Establishing intentions as a parent is a pivotal step in the realm of fatherhood. Each parenting path is unique, shaped not only by the needs and personalities of your children but also by your values, beliefs, and aspirations. Your approach holds immense influence over your child's growth and development, making it imperative to define your intentions and principles, creating a nurturing environment within your family.

Begin by delving into your values and beliefs. Consider what holds significance for you and how these principles align with your role as a father. These values become the bedrock upon which you build your parenting style, guiding your choices, responses, and interactions with your child. By understanding your core values, you can ensure that your parenting approach remains authentic and harmonious with your convictions.

Contemplate the lessons you aim to impart to your child. Think about the values you aspire to instill in their character, such as empathy, resilience, kindness, or a strong work ethic. These qualities lay the foundation for their future. Intentionally nurturing them can significantly contribute to your child's growth and well-being.

Consider also the kind of relationship you wish to foster with your child. Reflect upon the dynamics you hope to establish. Do you envision an open and communicative relationship where your child feels at ease sharing their thoughts and feelings?

Setting intentions for the bond you aim to create can guide your actions and interactions as a father.

DAD'S WORKOUT

- Prepare for a Ferris wheel of feelings with more plot twists than a soap opera.
- Set intentions for fatherhood but be ready to improvise —kids have a knack for throwing curveballs.
- Recognize that feeling excitement, uncertainty, and responsibility is normal—it's called "freaking the fuck out with big life changes, but you got this."

Exercise

As an upcoming father, it's beneficial to engage in a reflective exercise to prepare for this significant journey. Picture yourself cradling a newborn in your arms—take note of the emotions and thoughts that flood your mind. Reflect on your own experiences with your father—identify aspects you'd like to incorporate into your parenting style and areas you might want to modify. Consider the core beliefs you want to uphold as a father. Think about someone in your life with whom you could openly discuss these thoughts and feelings. Finally, outline a plan for self-education to equip yourself for the big day, embracing the responsibilities and joys of fatherhood.

CHAPTER 2
FIRST TRIMESTER: SUPPORTING YOUR PARTNER AND UNDERSTANDING THE CHANGES

> *A good father is one of the most unsung, unpraised, unnoticed, and yet one of the most valuable assets in our society.*
>
> BILLY GRAHAM

Welcome to the wild world of pregnancy! Your partner is about to embark on a rollercoaster ride of physical and emotional changes, and guess what? You're coming along you lucky guy! We'll help you master the art of being the ultimate partner and future parent, while also surviving the ride and thriving in the process. Bonus tip: Learn how to negotiate pizza slices with your pregnant wife without endangering your relationship—or your life! Word of advice, don't ever take the last piece!

First off, be the guy who swoops in to save the day. You'll be assisting with chores and lending an empathetic ear. We're talking about becoming the best laundry-folding, dishwashing, and compassionate listening dude the world has ever seen! Next, you'll need to understand hormonal mood swings and emotional whirlwinds. Your superpower here is patience and being the rock your partner can cling to in the storm. Remember, you're the emotional equivalent of a cozy, warm blanket. Then, let's tackle morning sickness. Think of it as your partner's kryptonite. Your mission? Discover ways to make it more bearable and provide comfort during the not-so-heroic moments.

Your schedule is about to get packed with prenatal appointments. Take notes, ask questions, and show the medical world you mean business. You also need to have open discussions about parenting—think of it as you're the quarterback in the huddle guiding the team to their next touchdown. Share your expectations, values, and beliefs about raising the little one. It's all part of developing your ultimate parenting game plan. Finally, prepare to gain confidence. Dive into hands-on experiences as you get ready for fatherhood. You might not be able to throw that 60-yard TD pass, but changing diapers and soothing a fussy baby are feats in their own right.

UNDERSTANDING PHYSICAL CHANGES

Emotional Changes and Hormones

Pregnancy is a tidal wave of emotion, where you'll navigate more ups and downs than a theme park ride. As the partner, your support is the secret sauce to keeping her on the pregnancy rollercoaster without losing her lunch. Your constant support helps make the rollercoaster more manageable.

Your mission, should you choose to accept it, is to create a safe space for your wife to unleash. Whether it's tears of joy, fear of the unknown, or pure happiness, let her feelings flow freely. Don't take her mood swings personally, and don't be shocked if she's suddenly crying over the last slice of pizza or ready to wrestle with the remote to change to the Bravo channel.

Listen Actively

Let's discuss the importance of being a good listener. Pregnancy can be overwhelming, and sometimes all your partner needs is someone to talk to. Be an active listener without immediately offering solutions. Let her know that you are there to lend an ear and genuinely understand what she is experiencing.

Reassurance and Comfort

This is the time to shower your wife with compliments and affection. Pregnancy can bring about moments of self-doubt and body image concerns, so don't hold back. Tell her that she is beautiful and show your love through gestures like hugs, kisses, and holding hands. Prego sex isn't bad either!

Patience Is Key

Hormones can lead to mood swings, and it is crucial not to react negatively. Stay patient and understanding during those moments—your calm presence can be incredibly soothing. Or, if you're going to lose your cool, find an outlet. Leave the situation with your wife in a positive manner and then relieve that built-up tension elsewhere (in a healthy way, of course!)

Active Participation

Here's another tip—actively participate in the pregnancy journey. Whenever possible, attend prenatal appointments and check-ups. It demonstrates your commitment and helps alleviate her anxiety, too. You don't have to read a 1,000-page day-by-day guide—just know the general situation and what's required.

Discussing Spiritual Beliefs

If your wife has spiritual beliefs, engage in meaningful conversations about them. Show genuine interest in how her beliefs connect with pregnancy and parenthood. It's an excellent way to provide emotional support while strengthening your connection (*7 Tips on How to Support Your Pregnant Wife*, 2022).

Planning Special Moments

Consider planning some special moments together. Grand, over-the-top gestures might not always cut it. Remember, pregnancy can be exhausting, and your wife is the real superhero here. But planning a date night or creating small, sweet moments can make her feel cherished. Just make sure to consult her on any plans.

Reflect on Your Journey

Time for a romantic stroll down memory lane, you lovebirds! Rewind to the beginning of your epic love story. Share stories about your journey as a couple, from your first meeting to this exciting phase of parenthood. It's a beautiful way to connect and prepare for the changes ahead. Remember that funny mishap on your first date? Or how you both got lost on that spontaneous road trip? Those inside jokes and shared adventures—they're the glue that holds you together.

Encourage Self-Care

Lastly, encourage self-care. Remind her to take breaks, relax, and indulge in self-care activities. Here's where you can sprinkle in some extra love: Surprise her with a bubble—filled, aromatic bath, complete with soothing music and dimmed lights. Or whip up her all-time favorite meal so she can savor every bite in peace.

Navigating Morning Sickness

During pregnancy, many women go through morning sickness and develop sensitivities to certain foods. To make your partner more comfortable, considerate actions are key. Avoid preparing or eating those specific foods around her to prevent any discomfort (Garzón, 2021). Now, let's talk about your breath— yes, you read that right. Certain smells, like those from beer or coffee, could trigger nausea if she notices them on your breath. By taking these measures, you can create a more comfortable environment for both of you.

Morning sickness during pregnancy can be quite the misnomer —it's like a surprise party guest who shows up unannounced at breakfast, lunch, or dinner, leaving you wondering if your stomach got the invitation memo!

So, what's this sickness all about? Well, it typically shows up as that queasy, uneasy feeling in the stomach. Imagine feeling like you're on a ship in choppy waters, except it can happen anytime. Hormonal changes and a heightened sense of smell can trigger this delightful experience. If your partner is feeling unwell, here are some ways you can help:

- **Offer Ginger**: Ginger can work wonders when it comes to nausea. You can prepare ginger tea or offer ginger candies or ginger ale to your partner. It's a natural remedy that may provide some relief.

- **Crackers or Dry Toast**: Simple, bland foods like crackers or dry toast can help settle the stomach. Keep some on hand, especially by her bedside, so she can have a few before getting out of bed in the morning.
- **Peppermint**: Peppermint tea or candies may also help soothe nausea. The refreshing taste can be comforting when she's feeling queasy.
- **Small, Frequent Meals**: Encourage your partner to eat smaller, more frequent meals throughout the day. An empty stomach can exacerbate nausea, so having something in her belly can help.
- **Stay Hydrated**: Dehydration can worsen morning sickness. Ensure she's drinking plenty of water throughout the day. Sipping water slowly and using a straw can sometimes make it easier to keep fluids down.
- **Acupressure Bands**: Some women find relief by wearing acupressure bands, which apply pressure to specific points on the wrists that are believed to reduce nausea. It might just be the trick that makes her feel better during this time!
- **Avoid Trigger Foods**: Pay attention to foods that trigger her symptoms and avoid cooking or eating them in her presence. Strong-smelling or greasy foods are often culprits.
- **Fresh Air**: Encourage her to get some fresh air. Sometimes, stepping outside and taking slow, deep breaths can help alleviate nausea.
- **Rest**: Ensure she gets plenty of rest. Fatigue can worsen morning sickness, so encourage naps and early nights.

- **Consult a Healthcare Professional**: If her morning sickness is severe and persistent, consider consulting a healthcare professional. They can provide guidance and, in some cases, prescribe medication to help manage the symptoms.

Being a Supportive Partner

You're already acing it by seeking tips on being the best support system out there.

Attend Prenatal Appointments

Make it a priority to attend all prenatal appointments; it's crucial for your involvement and support during this important time. Take the opportunity to actively engage with the healthcare professionals, ask any questions that come to mind, and stay fully informed about the progress of the pregnancy. This is your chance to be her ultimate partner-in-crime and provide the necessary support and care throughout this exciting journey.

Stay Informed

It's time to hit the books! Take some time to dive into the nitty-gritty details of pregnancy, childbirth, and the postpartum period. The more you know, the more you can impress your partner with your newfound expertise, making you the designated expert in the room and the ultimate pregnancy aficionado.

Discussing Parenting Philosophies With Your Partner

As you prepare for fatherhood, is like entering a jungle of diverse parenting philosophies. These philosophies can differ significantly between individuals and can be influenced by various factors such as personal values, upbringing, and cultural backgrounds. To ensure a strong and effective parenting approach, have open and honest discussions with your partner about your expectations, values, and beliefs when it comes to raising a child. Remember, babies thrive on routine and consistency, so having a united front can help to support that and ultimately your baby.

Confidence in your parenting abilities is not something that happens overnight; the secret is to roll up your sleeves and dive into hands-on experience and practice. This practical experience will build a solid foundation from which you can nurture your child with assurance and adaptability. As you face the challenges of fatherhood, having this confidence will allow you to play an active and supportive role in your child's life.

DAD'S WORKOUT

- Pregnancy mood swings are a soap opera where the main character's emotions change faster than a channel flip.
- Providing emotional support during pregnancy is like being a professional listener, nodding and smiling as you navigate her labyrinth of feelings.

- Attending prenatal appointments is a secret mission with your partner, gathering intel for the impending baby invasion. Knowledge is your superpower!
- Delve into the great debate of discovering your baby's gender: To peek or not to peek? Considering a grand gender reveal? Just make sure you're both on the same page. As for us, we went all out with powdered golf balls – because why not add a dash of sporty suspense to the mix!

CHAPTER 3
SECOND TRIMESTER: BABY ON BOARD

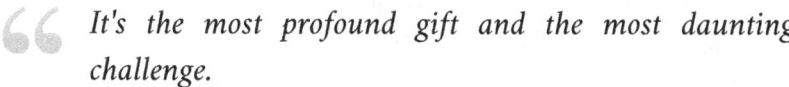 *It's the most profound gift and the most daunting challenge.*

MATT BOMER

The second trimester is an incredibly exciting time, often referred to as the "honeymoon phase." During these months, your baby undergoes remarkable transformations. This chapter will cover the journey of their development, their senses awakening, and the first signs of their little movements. Plus, you'll learn about the role of ultrasound imaging in keeping an eye on your baby's health and progress.

As the anticipation and excitement continue to grow, it's time to roll up your sleeves and plan the nursery together. You'll be assembling furniture and arranging all the baby essentials. This isn't just about comfort; it's also about preparing for the journey of parenthood. You'll also be delving into the world of baby gear. From strollers to cribs, you'll want to find the perfect fit for your family. Don't forget to consider the financial side of things, from budgeting for baby-related expenses to setting up a savings plan.

Insider trick: Don't buy the expensive stuff – throw a baby shower and ask for those as gifts.

Insider trick x2: Ask your friends with kids what they liked/didn't like, and what worked/didn't work. They can help you navigate the trillion-dollar baby industry and filter out the noise.

Now, when it comes to healthcare, it's time to make those arrangements for both your partner and the baby. That means scheduling appointments and selecting a pediatrician. And if you're thinking about daycare, don't procrastinate—good options tend to fill up quickly.

The birth experience: It's a show where you're not the head-liner, but your presence is needed for the success of the performance, aka you're the bass player. Educate yourself about the process, potential complications, and the choices available. Strong, open communication with your partner is key, and it's equally important to remain adaptable and open-minded about your birth plan. As concerns or fears arise, tackle them together and keep the intimacy alive—it might not always be physical, but emotional connection through communication, affection, and shared experiences is invaluable.

You might also consider taking birth preparation classes and familiarizing yourself with labor techniques to support your partner. Exploring the concept of a flexible birth plan is wise - babies have their own timeline. Lastly, a virtual tour of the hospital or birthing center will help you feel more at ease with the environment and logistics.

THE HONEYMOON PHASE

Oh, the second trimester, often referred to as the "honeymoon phase" of pregnancy! As a father, consider this your perfect opportunity to enjoy moments of blissful anticipation. Here's why the second trimester is the dad's version of a honeymoon:

Goodbye Morning Sickness, Hello Breakfast Celebrations: Bid farewell to the horrors of morning sickness during breakfast. Now, you can discuss the day's meal plan without worrying about potential projectile incidents. How about giving each other high-fives over pancakes?

An Energy Boost for Dad-ventures: It's not just a break for mom; it's a burst of energy for both of you. Suddenly, your partner is ready for fun—spontaneous weekend trips or game-day cookouts, perhaps?

No More Wardrobe Battles: Take a break from the struggle with maternity clothes. During the second trimester, your partner might even consider wearing non-stretchy pants again. It's a hello to buttons and zippers, my friends!

The Baby Bump Becomes a Belly Beacon: The baby bump goes from being mistaken for a big lunch to clearly showing that a little human is growing inside. Your partner's belly becomes a magnet for excited pats, adorable baby talk, and, of course, belly selfies. However, be prepared for those weirdos who approach wanting to touch your wife's belly – we politely declined a few proposals there.

Mood Swings Settle Down (Mostly): The emotional roller-coaster takes a break, and you no longer have to tiptoe around potential emotional outbursts. The second trimester feels more like watching a sitcom, with more predictable emotions. Well, for the most part; still don't take the last slice of pizza if you know what's good for you.

Foodie Freedom (with Limits): Cravings become less surprising and more like a manageable challenge. You can finally stock the fridge without fearing a late-night snack request involving peanut butter and anchovies.

Planning the Perfect Babymoon: With the storm of first-trimester symptoms behind you, it's time to plan the ultimate babymoon. Look for a destination that promises relaxation, a fully stocked mini-fridge, and a cozy pillow fort for those inevitable pregnancy nap sessions. We can't stress this enough! Take a final, celebratory trip as a child-less couple to kick back, relax, and get your mind right for what's to come.

So, dads, enjoy the glow of the second trimester. It's your time to shine, crack some dad jokes, and revel in the excitement before the third trimester brings a whole new level of adventure!

BABY'S DEVELOPMENT AND MILESTONES

Fetal Growth

Your baby goes through some amazing growth and changes during the second trimester. Think of it as a transformation from a tiny, almost invisible creature to a small human being. At the start of this trimester, your baby is still pretty small, maybe the size of a lemon. But as time goes on, they grow rapidly. By the end of the second trimester, they're about as long as a big banana, weighing around 1.5 to 2.5 pounds (*Second Trimester- Baby's Growth and Changes in You*, 2023). This is when you start seeing those cute little fingers, toes, and even some soft hair.

What's even more incredible is that during these months, the major organs like the heart, lungs, liver, and kidneys are hard at work. While they might not be fully mature yet, they're doing their job. Your baby's skin starts looking more like baby skin, and they might even have a few eyelashes and eyebrows. Those little bones are getting stronger, and muscles are developing, so they can start moving more. Speaking of movement, this is when you might start feeling your baby's tiny kicks and flutters, which is an unforgettable experience for parents.

But there's more to it—your baby's senses are also starting to wake up. They can hear sounds from the outside world, so talking to them is a great way to bond. It's amazing how they might respond to your voice with some wiggles. Or, start playing some music for them! We are musicians and enjoyed playing music while our little one was in Mama's belly dancing away!

So, this trimester is like the "coming soon" trailer of your baby's blockbuster debut, where they're transforming from a tiny prop to a leading actor in this grand production. And you? You're prepping for the adventure of parenthood, ready to tackle plot twists, sleepless nights, and those inevitable diaper change scenes with all the enthusiasm of a first-time director!

Sensory Development

The baby's sensory experiences and stimuli in the womb are important for their preparation to adapt to the outside world after birth. During the second trimester, development sets the groundwork for further sensory refinement and maturation in the third trimester and beyond. Let's see what incredible acts your fetus is cooking up in its tiny, aquatic studio during this phase:

- **Hearing:** Around the 16th week, the fetus can begin to hear external sounds, such as the mother's heartbeat, blood circulation, and even some muffled sounds from the external environment (Boyd-Barrett, 2021). The sense of hearing continues to improve throughout the trimester, with the baby becoming more responsive to noises.
- **Taste:** Taste buds develop around the 14th week, and the fetus begins to swallow and digest the amniotic fluid (de Bellefonds, 2021). The flavors of the amniotic

fluid can be influenced by the mother's diet, exposing the fetus to different tastes. This early experience with flavors can potentially influence the baby's food preferences after birth.

- **Touch:** The second trimester marks the development of more advanced sensory receptors in the skin, allowing the fetus to respond to various forms of tactile stimulation such as gentle strokes or pressure on the mother's abdomen.

- **Vision:** While the eyes continue to develop in the second trimester, the fetus's vision is limited due to the darkness of the womb. The eyes remain closed during this time, and the baby's visual experience primarily consists of perceiving changes in light and shadow, as well as sensing the warmth and darkness of the womb.

- **Olfaction (Smell):** Although the sense of smell is developing, it is less prominent in the womb. The fetus can still inhale and be exposed to some scents in the amniotic fluid, but it plays a smaller role compared to other senses like hearing and touch.

Movement and Playfulness

As the fetus's muscles and nervous system mature, it becomes more active and responsive to stimuli. The baby's movements become more coordinated, and the mother may start to feel the fluttering of fetal movements during this trimester. Your little one is now capable of stretching, sucking their thumb, yawning, and displaying adorable facial expressions (*Baby Development Month by Month*, 2019).

Ultrasound Imaging

During this time, the reproductive organs develop significantly, and this is when the genitals become distinguishable. An ultrasound can be used to visualize these organs, which are crucial in determining the baby's sex. The second trimester often involves a comprehensive ultrasound examination called the anatomy scan, which is usually conducted between the 18th and 22nd weeks of pregnancy (*20 Week Ultrasound*, n.d.). This allows healthcare providers to assess the baby's overall health and development. In addition to the reproductive organs, the scan also checks various other structures and systems such as the heart, brain, spine, kidneys, and limbs. It can help identify any potential issues that may require further attention or monitoring.

Ultrasound technology also provides information about the baby's position and movements. Expectant parents can witness their baby's activities, such as kicking, stretching, and sometimes even sucking their thumb. This can be a heartwarming and reassuring experience as they get a glimpse of their growing child's behavior inside the womb. Additionally, the second-trimester ultrasound offers valuable insights into the baby's growth and development. Measurements of head circumference, limb length, and overall size provide an estimate of the baby's gestational age and ensure that they are progressing as expected.

PREPARING FOR THE ARRIVAL

Nursery Planning

Nursery planning is the fun pregame to your baby's home opener! It's where you get to unleash your creative side and make sure everything's safe and cozy for your little one. Team up with your partner for some brainstorming sessions. You'll want to talk about what themes and colors you want to sprinkle into your baby's world. Think about stuff that'll make your little explorer's eyes sparkle and maybe help them learn a thing or two while they're at it. Oh, and don't forget the furniture and gear—a crib, a changing table, and all those storage solutions and baby monitors (Attygalla, 2022).

Doing all this with your partner is not just about getting the job done; it's about turning the prep work into a bonding experience and a sneak peek of the teamwork you're about to do as parents. You're not just putting up cute decorations—you're setting the stage for love and care to shine through every corner.

Plus, nursery planning is a great way to get you ready for parenthood. It's your way of showing your commitment to providing the best environment for your child. It's not just about aesthetics; it's about safety, practicality, and making sure everything can adapt as your baby grows. This isn't just fun and games; it's filling your baby's first moments at home with care. Making sure your home is baby-friendly, or "dad-proofing," is a way dads show their love for their new bundle of joy by keeping them safe and sound.

Baby Gear

This is the ideal moment to dive into researching and planning for all the must-have stuff for when your baby comes into the picture. Think about everything from baby strollers and cribs to car seats and diapers—it's a whole world to explore! Take some time to browse through reviews, compare prices, and chat with your friends and family to get their input. Doing all of this will make sure you're fully ready and stocked up when your little bundle of joy finally arrives. Oh, and keep an eye on your wallet too, because some baby gear can dig into your budget.

Must-Have Baby Items Checklist

Sleep

- Baby crib: A safe bed for your baby.
- Co-sleeper or bassinet: A smaller bed for your baby, perfect for your room. Consider a crib that includes a rocking motion or built-in white noise. This helped us promote good sleep with our newborn. It's so worth it!
- Swaddle blankets: Blankets to wrap your baby for comfort.
- Zip-up baby swaddles: Easy-to-use swaddles for better sleep. We'd recommend the zip kind as they are much easier to use.
- Sound machine (white noise): Creates soothing sounds for better sleep. **100% get a sound machine!**
- Pacifier: Helps with self-soothing.
- Crib mattress: Comfortable mattress for the crib.
- Baby monitor: Keeps an eye on your baby.
- Smart sock monitor: Monitors baby's sleep and health.

Feeding (Breastfeeding)

- Nursing bras: Comfortable bras for breastfeeding.
- Nursing pads: Absorbent pads to prevent leaks.
- Breastfeeding pillow: Supports comfortable nursing.
- Nipple balm: Helps soothe and protect nipples.
- Silicone breast pump: Efficient and portable.
- Electric breast pump: Efficient milk extraction.

- Hands-free pumping bra: Convenient for hands-free pumping.

Feeding (Bottle-Feeding & Solids)

- Baby bottles: Containers for feeding.
- Bottle brush: Cleans baby bottles.
- Drying rack: Allows baby bottle parts to air dry.
- Burp cloths: Absorbent cloths to prevent mess.
- Formula dispenser: Convenient formula feeding.
- High chair: Provides a safe space for feeding.
- First foods feeding set: Essentials for starting solids.
- Utensils: Baby-friendly utensils.
- Sippy cups: Training cups for older babies.

On-the-Go

- Car seat: Essential for safe travel.
- Travel crib: Portable bed for travel.
- Portable sleep pod: Creates a dark sleep environment.
- Stroller: For easy transportation.
- Diaper bag: Carries baby essentials. Look for a unisex version unless you want to feel glamorous.
- Baby carriers (various types): Keeps baby close on the go.

Clothing

- Onesies: Basic baby outfits. Get zip onesies—button ones suck when you're trying to change diapers.
- Baby hats: Keeps baby's head warm.
- Socks: Keeps baby's feet warm.
- Mittens: Prevents baby from scratching.

Newborn Care

- Diapers: Essential for hygiene.
- Baby wipes: For cleaning and diaper changes.
- Wipe dispenser: Convenient wipe access.
- Diaper rash cream: Prevents and soothes diaper rash.
- Diaper pail: Contains diaper odors. Get one that closes cause those smells are for real.
- Changing pad: Provides a clean changing surface.
- Nail clippers or trimmers: Safely trim baby's nails.
- Baby teether/toothbrush: For oral care.

Bath Time

- Baby bathtub: For safe bathing.
- Inflatable infant bather: Supports baby during bath.
- Baby shampoo and wash: Gentle cleaning products.
- Bath rinser: Makes hair washing easier.
- Hooded towels and washcloths: Keeps baby warm.
- Baby lotion: Hydrates baby's skin.
- Bath toys: Entertainment during bath time.

Play

- Activity center: Keeps baby engaged.
- Teething toys: Soothe teething discomfort.
- Crinkle books: Introduces babies to books.
- Rattles: Auditory stimulation.
- Play mat or activity gym: Safe play area.
- Baby swing: Calming motion for baby.
- Bouncer: Soothing vibrations.

Health & Safety

- Nasal aspirator: Clears baby's nasal passages.
- Saline nasal spray: Helps with congestion.
- First aid kit: Essential for minor injuries.
- Rectal thermometer: Accurate temperature readings.
- Forehead thermometer: Quick temperature checks.

Financial Preparations

Take a close look at your current financial situation. Start by assessing your income, expenses, savings, and any existing debts. This helps you understand your financial baseline. Once you have a clear picture of where you stand, it's time to create a budget tailored to accommodate the additional expenses that come with having a child.

Your budget should include a breakdown of expected costs related to your new family member. This encompasses essentials like baby supplies, medical expenses associated with prenatal care and childbirth, potential childcare costs, and adjustments for parental leave income changes. Do you have healthcare coverage? Think of this budget as your financial roadmap for the upcoming months and years. It's not just about covering immediate costs, though. Consider long-term financial goals like saving for your child's education and ensuring you have a financial safety net, like an emergency fund, for unexpected expenses. This is also the time to talk about updating or establishing your will and life insurance (Sillers, 2021). Also, people are always wanting to get rid of baby stuff—reach out to friends for cheap donations or post on social media if you need anything.

Healthcare Arrangements

- **Know Your Health Insurance**: First off, dive into your health insurance policy and figure out what's covered when it comes to those baby-related expenses. Look out for things like copays, deductibles (those costs you gotta pay before insurance kicks in), and any limits that might affect how much you pay for your partner's prenatal care and birthing process.
- **Prenatal Care**: Next up, it's all about those prenatal care appointments. These are super important for keeping an eye on your partner's health and ensuring a smooth pregnancy journey. It involves a bunch of

doctor visits, tests, and those cool ultrasound pics to track how your little one is doing.

- **Find a Pediatrician**: The baby's doctor, aka the pediatrician, is a big deal. You'll want to do some research and find one who vibes with your family's style and values. This doctor will be in charge of all those baby check-ups, shots, and making sure your little one is happy and healthy. Don't forget to set up an initial meeting with the pediatrician before the big day to chat about any questions or worries you might have.
- **Paperwork Prowess**: Finally, don't underestimate the power of paperwork. This includes filling out those birth certificate forms at the hospital and snagging your baby's Social Security Number. It's not just about bureaucracy; it's for things like tax perks and making sure your baby can access all the important stuff they need. So, get that paperwork game strong!

Daycare

It is extremely important to start your search for a daycare for your child as early as possible. Daycare centers often have limited space and fill up quickly with other parents. Therefore, if you plan to use daycare services, it is crucial to begin your search well in advance.

Think of it like trying to get tickets to a popular concert or a limited event. The earlier you start looking, the better chance you have of securing a spot that meets your needs and preferences. By starting your search early, you give yourself more time to research and visit different daycare options, ask important questions, and ultimately find the perfect fit for your child. The goal is to avoid any last-minute rushes or settling for a daycare that may not be the best match for your child. You'll want to be sure the daycare is safe, provides ample attention based upon teacher-to-student ratio, and engages in active development – be picky here and don't settle. It's like a second mortgage, so make sure it's worth your money.

BIRTH PREPARATION AND CLASSES

Giving birth is a profoundly significant and emotional experience in your partner's life. Childbirth is not just about the physical process they are going through but also about her feelings, the connection between you both, and the transformation into parenthood. It's entirely normal for either of you to feel intense joy, nervousness, and even fear. What can help is running through the process—either thinking of each step, writing down your plan, or going through the motions—when she starts to give birth, what do you do? That can be the most daunting feeling, but prepping for it and knowing the motions can help alleviate that worry.

Think of childbirth like a big exam. You wouldn't walk into a test without studying, right? So, it's essential to learn about the whole birthing process, what could go differently than expected, and what choices you might have. This way, you're ready for any surprises that might come up. Knowledge is power, especially when it comes to childbirth. Taking classes can provide valuable insights into what to expect, and how to make informed decisions. Being well-informed can help reduce anxiety and give you a sense of control during a time that can otherwise feel unpredictable. Openly discuss your expectations and any fears with your partner. Having these conversations helps both of you to be on the same page and provide the support that's needed during labor.

Remaining Flexible and Open-Minded About Your Plans

Everyone has their unique preferences and hopes for how they want their childbirth experience to unfold. Whether it's about pain relief options like epidurals, decisions about saving or donating cord blood, or even considering keeping the placenta for encapsulation, there's a lot to think about (Cassell, 2021).

However, even the most detailed plans can take unexpected turns. That's where being adaptable comes in. Your role as a partner is to be supportive and make decisions with the woman in labor in mind. Sometimes, you might need to change course based on what's happening in the moment. This is where you might shrug your shoulders, make an informed decision, and roll with the changes.

MANAGING CHANGES IN YOUR RELATIONSHIP DURING THIS TRANSFORMATIVE TIME

Managing the changes in your relationship during the shift to parenthood is like learning how to play a new board game. While you'll encounter concerns and fears, instead of flipping the board in frustration, you work together to find clever solutions.

So, when those questions and worries pop up—like who's on laundry duty or how to handle the ever-growing list of baby expenses—have a good chat. You don't need to be experts; it's more about making the effort to work as a dynamic duo. And who knows, you might even discover that parenthood comes with a hidden talent for making quirky baby noises or rocking mismatched socks!

Maintaining Intimacy

Just so you know, your partner's sex drive can be all over the place during pregnancy—it can even change from one trimester to the next. It can get a bit confusing with all the changes her body's going through. Some folks might feel like they're ready to set new records for intimacy, while others might be like, "Mood? What's that?" There are loads of reasons for this, from being super tired, feeling queasy, to not feeling great about her changing body, and even worrying about the little one on the way (Lindberg, n.d.).

That being said, this is a great time to focus on maintaining emotional intimacy. You know, through communication, affection, and shared experiences. Sometimes, the real connection is more about those moments when you laugh together, cuddle up on the couch, or just chat about your day.

OPTIONAL THINGS TO CONSIDER

Choosing Birth Classes

So, there are these birth preparation classes out there, with different techniques like Lamaze, Bradley, and Hypnobirthing. They're like different flavors of ice cream. Each has its own unique benefits, so check them out with your partner and pick the one that feels like the best fit for you both. It's like choosing the flavor you both love!

Labor Techniques

You may want to learn relaxation, breathing, and pain management techniques that can be super helpful for your partner during labor. Get some strategies into your playbook for game day!

Birth Plan

Creating a birth plan can help address the numerous questions that arise during childbirth. It's hard to concentrate while your partner is in pain during labor. A birth plan is essentially a written document that outlines your partner's desired preferences and wishes for the delivery and labor process of your child. It typically includes key information such as the birthing environment, pain management, and preferred medical interventions, if necessary. The purpose is to effectively communicate your partner's preferences to healthcare providers and ensure that the entire birthing experience aligns with their values and desires. However, babies tend to be unpredictable. A flexible birth plan that reflects your partner's desires while also being prepared for unexpected scenarios is more realistic. Think of it more like a loose guiding document rather than a strict set of instructions.

Hospital Tour

If you're the kind of person who likes to know the layout of the stadium before going to the big game, take a virtual tour of the hospital or birthing center. This way, you and your partner can get familiar with the place and how things work.

Babymoon Planning

With the storm of first-trimester symptoms behind you, the second trimester is the perfect time to plan a babymoon. Go somewhere relaxing before the baby arrives and enjoy the luxury of sleeping without a newborn-induced alarm clock.

DAD'S WORKOUT

- Embrace your inner modern dad: The stroller is your new chariot, and baby wipes are your secret weapon.
- Embark on the dad-venture: Survive prenatal classes and assemble cribs like a pro.
- Join the Dad-Bod Revolution! It represents your dedication to being a parent.

CHAPTER 4
THIRD TRIMESTER: COUNTDOWN TO PARENTHOOD

 Fatherhood is the best thing I ever did. It changes your perspective.

BRAD PITT

As the due date draws near, you can't help but feel more and more excited about meeting your little one. This chapter focuses on the important aspects of the last few months before your baby arrives. It will provide you with the necessary knowledge and skills for parenting and help you prepare for the journey of parenthood. You'll revisit your list of baby essentials, create an emergency contact list, finalize work arrangements, prepare freezer meals, and even plan for unexpected situations by having a hospital bag ready to go. Review and discuss your birth plan, take a tour of the hospital or birthing center if you haven't done so already, and become familiar with the guidelines for visitors. Finally, we address managing anxiety and excitement, embracing the unknown, and supporting each other through the mix of emotions that come with this final trimester.

FINAL PREPARATIONS

As we're getting closer to the big day, it's prime time to make sure we're all set for the baby's arrival. Here's the deal:

- **Baby Essentials:** Let's double-check our list of must-have baby items. Diapers, baby clothes, feeding gear— we want to have it all sorted.
- **Emergency Contacts:** Prepare a list of important contacts. That includes our healthcare provider, birthing coach, and trusted family or friends who can back us up during labor.
- **Maternity Leave and Work:** Don't forget about work arrangements. Finalize the plan for your partner's maternity leave and any paternity leave you'll be taking. Also, ensure your workplace is in the loop.
- **Meal Prep:** Think about doing some meal prep and stocking up the freezer. Trust me, having ready-to-go meals can be a lifesaver in those hectic early days of parenthood when cooking isn't a top priority.
- **Hospital Game Plan:** Let's figure out the logistics of getting to the hospital and know exactly where to go. Emergencies can happen, so having that hospital bag packed and ready is a smart move.

HOSPITAL LOGISTICS AND BIRTH PLANS

Hospital Bag Packing

When it comes to packing your hospital bag, it's important to be organized and prepared. Both you and your partner will need some essentials during your stay, so creating a checklist is a great idea. There is a good chance you'll be at the hospital for at least a couple of days, so packing everything you need is important. We were there for a total of five days, and luckily, when we weren't sleeping from three days of labor, we had everything we needed since we packed accordingly.

Start by packing comfortable clothes for yourself. Opt for loose, breathable outfits that will make you feel at ease. Don't forget to include toiletries, such as toothbrushes, toothpaste, shampoo, and soap, to help you feel refreshed.

Remember to include snacks in your bag. Hunger can strike at any time and having some nourishing treats will be greatly appreciated. Granola bars, nuts, and dried fruits are all great options to have on hand.

Next, gather all the important documents that you may need during your hospital stay. This includes your identification, health insurance information, and any necessary paperwork from your healthcare provider. Having these documents readily available will make the check-in process much smoother.

Consider bringing a tablet or a book to help pass the time during labor or recovery. And of course, don't forget to pack your phone charger to ensure that you can stay connected with loved ones and capture those precious, or not-so-precious, moments.

Now let's shift the focus to your little one. Take the initiative to pack a few things for your baby as well. Start by selecting a onesie or an outfit for them to wear when coming home for the first time. Babies can't regulate their body temperature as adults do, so don't forget to include a tiny hat and mittens to ensure they stay warm and cozy.

Birth Plan Revisited

Remember that birth plan you put together in the second trimester? Well, now's the time to dust it off. Sit down with your healthcare provider and go through it again. Make sure what you want aligns with how the hospital does things.

Hospital Tour

If you haven't done so already, it's a good idea to schedule an in-person or virtual tour of the hospital or birthing center where you plan to give birth. This will allow you to become familiar with the layout, parking, and entrances of the facility. Being prepared and knowing where to go when labor begins can help reduce stress and confusion. Plan your route to the hospital and consider any potential traffic or road conditions so that you can arrive promptly. Knowing these details ahead of time can provide peace of mind and ensure a smoother experience when the time comes.

Visitor Guidelines

Take the time to familiarize yourself with the hospital's rules and regulations regarding visitors and be sure to communicate these rules to your friends and family. You might not want to have a bunch of people in the waiting room. It can be helpful to have a plan in place so that everyone involved knows what to expect. If you need to, designate someone to be the family bouncer to ensure you're not overwhelmed when the baby arrives – perhaps allocate this to the "bossy" one in the family.

DEALING WITH ANXIETY AND EXCITEMENT

Managing Anxiety

Major life changes like becoming a father can't be entirely prepared for, and it's okay to feel anxious about it. However, there are positive ways to manage this anxiety. Quick mindfulness exercises can be really helpful. For example, try box breathing: Inhale for 4 seconds, hold for 4 seconds, exhale for 4 seconds, and hold for 4 seconds. Repeat this exercise for a couple of minutes, and you'll notice that it significantly slows down your heart rate and helps you calm down. If breathing exercises aren't your thing, consider meeting up with a friend who has already gone through this experience. Grabbing lunch and discussing their experience as a father can put things into perspective and make you feel less alone in your worries and anxieties. Lastly, sometimes you just need a little break. It's completely fine to have a beer and take a moment to zone out and relax. We've been there practicing this fine art in moderation.

Communication

It's true—most guys say what needs to be said and that's about it. However, it might be beneficial to express those suppressed emotions as a means of managing the stress and anxiety that come with planning the birthing process. There is so much to learn and handle, and simply talking about it and sharing how you feel can help alleviate some of the burden. Remember, your partner is experiencing the same emotions, so feel free to connect with them over these shared feelings. If you have buddies who have gone through the same process, reach out to them and open up. Or, at least from our experience, soon-to-be grandparents are pumped and ready to spoil the little one—they are invested as well and can be good sounding boards.

Embracing the Unknown

As we mentioned before, no one can ever fully prepare themselves for what lies ahead—you can follow our advice in this book and become extremely well-prepared to be an excellent father, but there will always be an element of uncertainty. Despite any claims made by other resources about being completely "ready for the big day," it's normal to feel anxious as the birth approaches. This is the time to summon your inner dad spirit, the guy who's ready to face the unknown with confidence and strength. Simply acknowledging that these feelings are natural, finding ways to manage their impact, and accepting that flexibility and adaptability will be necessary, you will be able to overcome any challenges that come your way. Now, go pack your bag, fine-tune your game plan, and know that you will be a kick-ass father who can handle whatever comes your way.

DAD'S WORKOUT

- Packing your hospital bag is just the same as preparing for a camping trip where snacks, entertainment, and essential documents are your survival kit for the baby's grand entrance.
- Revisiting your birth plan is like going over the script with your director (the healthcare provider) to ensure your performance aligns with the hospital's stage.
- Planning for visitors during your hospital stay? You're orchestrating a backstage pass list for the grand show, letting everyone know when to cheer and when to wait in the wings.

CHAPTER 5
LABOR & DELIVERY
(PART TWO: THE BIG DAY)

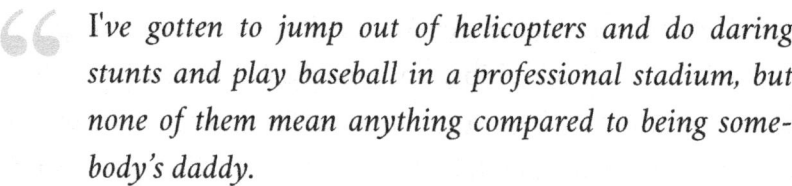

I've gotten to jump out of helicopters and do daring stunts and play baseball in a professional stadium, but none of them mean anything compared to being some-body's daddy.

CHRIS PRATT

The big day is just around the corner—the day your little one will make their grand entrance into the world. We're here to guide you through labor and delivery, but before we dive in, let us drop a pearl of wisdom from experience: Grab some shuteye whenever you can! Believe us, finding a moment to rest can be as elusive as a rare gem amidst the whirlwind of pregnancy and the first few hours after childbirth. If your delivery is anything like ours, you'll have only a couple of hours' sleep over several days—so get that rest when you can!

Now, let's talk about labor. Your role during this journey is crucial. You can be her rock, providing comfort and emotional support. But be ready for anything—from offering soothing words to witnessing moments you'd rather not see again. Sometimes you're her superhero, and other times, you might feel like you're driving her crazy.

You'll learn how to be there for her both physically and emotionally. Holding her hand, soothing words, and being her anchor during contractions—that's your game. You'll also pick up techniques like massage, counterpressure, and breathing to help her through the discomfort.

You've got to be her advocate, too, ensuring her birth preferences are communicated to the healthcare team. Keep her fueled with water, ice chips, and snacks because every bit of attention matters. When your baby arrives, you'll witness the miraculous moment they take their first breath. Depending on hospital policies, you might even get to cut the umbilical cord, marking your connection to your baby's birth. And here's a heads up: You'll likely hold your baby immediately after birth, which is amazing but can feel a tad daunting.

Now, skin-to-skin contact—that's a game-changer. It promotes bonding, warmth, and sets the stage for breastfeeding. If your partner chooses to breastfeed, be her biggest cheerleader. Help her find a comfortable position and offer support. If you're struggling with the initial stages of breastfeeding, don't hesitate to ask a nurse for guidance. They're the pros, and they're there to help.

SUPPORTING HER DURING LABOR

Make sure to get plenty of rest during pregnancy and after, as you will be up for long periods of time. This applies to both you and the mother. One thing they don't often tell you is that after giving birth, you'll be awake and moving around for the next 3-5 hours. So, if you're expecting to hand the baby over to the hospital daycare as soon as they are born and then get back to supporting the mother and getting some sleep, think again!

When we were coming back from the birth, we anticipated that a nurse would take the baby for a couple of hours and let us recoup. However, to our surprise, we were thrown directly into trying to breastfeed. Talk about a challenge we've never experienced before! We were beyond sleep-deprived, slightly delirious, and expected to try breastfeeding a newborn only an hour or so old. It was an impossible task and we didn't succeed; actually, our baby never breastfed and never latched. Just know going into the experience that you may encounter something similar and it could be a challenge. From the dad's perspective, this is a time when you have to manage your emotions and remain collected. The mom will be recovering from the birth and will need your support. We'll always remember this dad, determined to help the baby latch, resorting to a syringe to draw milk from the breast, and, in the process, accidentally pressing the alarm button. Here's to sharing a good laugh about it in the future!

Labor is a transformative and demanding experience for both the mother and her partner. Your role is crucial, as your support and presence can significantly impact her overall comfort and emotional well-being. You can offer valuable assistance and guidance throughout the labor process, making a meaningful difference in creating a positive and empowering birth experience.

Active Presence

Be there for her both physically and emotionally. Hold her hand, offer reassuring words, and be her unwavering support through the ups and downs of contractions. Chances are, she'll either want you by her side, feeling comforted, or she might be in a lot of pain and unintentionally direct her discomfort toward you. It's all part of the process, and your steadfast presence is key. You might witness or hear things that seem intense or distressing, but remember, it's all part of the journey, and it'll be worth it in the end. Be ready for the moment the baby arrives! They will hand you the baby right after birth, which can be an emotional and joyous experience. Embrace the moment and be prepared for this incredible first connection.

Comfort Measures

Familiarize yourself with various comfort techniques, such as massaging, applying counterpressure, and practicing breathing exercises. Some women like a fan blowing on them during labor, and you can offer her sips of water. These methods can greatly alleviate her discomfort and help make the labor process more manageable.

- **Massaging**: Massaging involves using gentle, rhythmic movements on the body, usually the back, shoulders, or other areas where the laboring woman may feel tension or discomfort. It helps to relax the muscles and can provide pain relief.
- **Counterpressure**: Counterpressure is a technique where pressure is applied to specific points on the body to alleviate pain or discomfort. It's often used on the lower back during labor to help ease the pressure and pain associated with contractions.
- **Breathing Exercises**: Breathing exercises are specific patterns of breathing that can help the laboring woman stay focused, relaxed, and manage pain during contractions. These techniques are aimed at maintaining a steady and calming rhythm to reduce stress and discomfort.

Advocate

It's really important to know your partner's birth preferences and be her champion during labor and delivery. Keep her birth plan handy and go through it so you understand what she wants. Your job of conveying her wishes to the healthcare team is a big deal—you're her voice when she can't speak! Being her advocate isn't just about making sure her birth experience matches her dreams; it's also about being there to provide the care and comfort she needs during this extraordinary moment in her life.

Hydration and Nutrition

Offer her water, ice chips, and snacks to help maintain her energy levels throughout labor. Your attentiveness can have a significant impact on her stamina and overall well-being. Keep in mind that certain medications, like an epidural, might limit your partner's ability to eat, but it's always okay for her to have water. Snacks will likely not be the traditional snack; you'll likely be making bone broth or giving her popsicles.

Breastfeeding

While it might be challenging to get the baby to breastfeed immediately, don't panic or hit the emergency button. Seek assistance from a nurse whom you feel comfortable with during labor. They have experience and can guide you through the initial steps after birth. Don't pretend to know it all; rely on their expertise for a smoother start to your breastfeeding journey.

WELCOMING YOUR BABY

New dad, when your baby arrives, it's an unforgettable moment. It's the start of a new chapter filled with love, joy, and endless possibilities. That first breath, that first cry—those are the real deal. Take a moment to soak it all in. In that room, there's so much love, happiness, and hope. It's a special, miraculous time, and it's something to celebrate. This section will walk you through the meaningful moments that come after the birth.

First Glimpse

There's an actual moment when you transition from partner to parent. Get ready for a life-altering experience as you witness your child's first breath and their entry into the world. You'll be hit with a rush of emotions, from joy and amazement to a profound sense of responsibility.

Cord Cutting

Depending on your preferences and hospital rules, you might have the chance to cut the umbilical cord. Include this in your birth plan. It's a symbolic act that connects you to this incredible birth experience.

Skin-to-Skin Contact

Holding your baby close immediately after birth is a game-changer. It fosters bonding, warmth, and helps kickstart breastfeeding. It's all about that physical connection, strengthening your emotional bond, and supporting your baby's early development. Dads can also enjoy the benefits of this practice by taking their shirt off. This is often referred to as "kangaroo care" because it mimics how kangaroos provide warmth and security to their babies (Steen, 2022). Hold your baby against your chest, providing warmth and comfort. Skin-to-skin contact promotes the formation of emotional connections and plays a vital role in the growth and development of your baby.

Supporting Breastfeeding

If your partner chooses to breastfeed, be her support system. Give her encouragement and a helping hand as she begins this journey. Assist her in finding a comfortable position and be there when she needs it. Teamwork is the name of the game, and sometimes it might involve some unique tasks to ensure your baby gets those vital nutrients right after birth. If she asks for your assistance in holding a breast or using a syringe to milk her immediately after birth, step up and lend a hand!

Embracing the Moment

Labor and delivery are incredible feats of strength and courage. Every birth story is one-of-a-kind, just like your own unique journey as a couple. Hold onto the love and unity that brought you to this moment. Staying fully engaged and savoring the moment can be challenging, as distractions often creep in. Make an effort to stay in the present and embrace every aspect of this experience.

DAD'S WORKOUT

- Labor support: Be there, offer comfort, and advocate for your partner's preferences.
- Welcoming your baby: Witness their birth, engage in moments like cord cutting, and encourage skin-to-skin contact and breastfeeding initiation.
- Embrace the uniqueness of each birth story and the powerful bond it forges between you and your partner.

MAKE A DIFFERENCE WITH YOUR REVIEW

UNLOCK THE POWER OF DAD WISDOM

"Helping others is like the ultimate superpower. You might not get a cape, but you'll get a whole lot of good karma."

DADDY BOOT CAMP

Ready to be a hero without the cape? Let's chat about something super important—making a real difference in a dad-to-be's life, just like you!

A Quick Question: Would you lend a hand to a dad you've never met, even if you didn't get a high-five for it? Picture this guy—it's a bit like you or the version of you who was new to the dad game. Eager to make a difference, needing help, and not quite sure where to start.

Our mission is simple: to make "First-Time Dad's Journey to Parenthood" a handbook for every dad out there. Everything we do is wrapped up in that mission. And the only way for us to make it happen is by reaching... well, everyone.

Here's Your Mission: Most people do judge a book by its cover (and, you guessed it, by its reviews). So, here's a favor to ask for a struggling dad-to-be you've never met:

Could you help that dad by leaving this book a review?

Your gift takes less than 60 seconds, costs nothing, but can change another expecting dad's life forever. Your review might help…

- Turn sleepless nights into restful victories
- Be Dad's daily dose of laughter
- Master the subtle art of understanding your baby's coos, cries, and giggles

Simply scan the QR code below to leave your review:

Thank you from the bottom of my heart. Now, back to our regularly scheduled dad-ventures!

Your biggest fan,

Daddy Boot Camp

CHAPTER 6
THE NEWBORN PHASE: SURVIVAL MODE
(PART THREE: EMBRACING FATHERHOOD)

> *Having children is like living in a frat house. Nobody sleeps, everything's broken, and there's a lot of throwing up.*

RAY ROMANO

Sleep is for the weak—or for those without a newborn. The arrival of your newborn marks a significant shift in your life, filled with moments of awe, joy, and, let's be honest, some challenging times. This chapter is your guide to navigating the initial challenges of the newborn phase and entering "survival mode." We'll cover everything from caring for your baby's needs to managing sleep deprivation and nurturing your relationship, helping you thrive during this transformative period.

The first few months with a newborn are both intense and temporary. As you navigate through this phase, remember that every challenge presents an opportunity for growth and bonding. Embrace the small victories, lean on each other for support, and cherish this amazing time. Taking care of your baby involves a combination of joy and demanding tasks. Lack of sleep is a common issue for new parents and can be difficult to handle. The early days of parenthood may bring challenges to your relationship, but with intention and effort, it can also bring growth and a deeper connection.

BONDING THROUGH CAREGIVING

Being a first-time dad means mastering changing diapers and soothing a fussy little one. These skills empower you to be a hands-on dad in no time. Now, bear in mind that every child is a unique little puzzle, so be prepared for surprises along the way. A golden rule of dad wisdom: Don't forget the "ass cream." It's a baby's guard against diaper rash. If you've got a boy, watch out for surprise sprinklers—never stand with your head directly over the target area (McKay, 2013). Invest in a good trash can for all those "treasure-filled" diapers: one that seals tight and has a fancy slide. And here's a heads-up: There will be blowouts. And yes, they are exactly as disgusting as they sound.

Insider tip: Always carry an extra onesie with you. We've made the mistake of leaving home without one and having a blowout. Our little guy didn't enjoy the drive home in his diaper.

Infants have a limited understanding of the world around them and depend on their caregivers for all their needs. Although they don't start speaking verbally until they reach around 12 months old, they are still able to communicate effectively. They do this by conveying important information about their physical health and emotions through their body language. Learning to interpret these signals is like unlocking the secret language of parenthood. When you respond promptly, it builds trust and makes your baby feel secure.

Cues are like your baby's way of communicating their feelings and needs (*Learning Your Baby's Cues*, n.d.). They come in different forms, some indicating your baby is eager to engage and interact, while others suggest your baby might require a break or some rest. To decipher these cues, pay attention to your baby's actions and their immediate environment. This will help you understand what your baby is trying to express.

Feeding

When it comes to feeding your little one, there are a few things to keep in mind. Whether you're going the breastfeeding or bottle-feeding route, understanding those feeding cues and schedules is key. And here's the deal—feeding is a team effort. So, if your partner is leaning toward breastfeeding, fantastic. But if it doesn't work out, don't sweat it. Our kid thrived on formula; just make sure you're picking a good one. The brand we used was HiPP and we shipped it from Europe. We chose this option because it contained wholesome, organic ingredients, aiming to give our baby a healthy start from the very beginning.

Now, the whole pumping thing—yeah, it can be a bit of a hassle, but it's worth it. It's like having a stash of baby gold in the freezer. Just know that sometimes, things like hypothyroidism and insufficient glandular tissue (IGT) can affect milk supply, so be prepared for that too.

When it's feeding time, get cozy with the little one, keep eye contact, and create a peaceful environment. This responsive feeding approach builds a sweet emotional connection during those precious moments. So, whether you're holding a bottle or offering the breast, it's all about bonding and nourishing your baby.

Babies use a variety of cues to communicate their hunger. Here are some common hunger cues in infants:

- **Rooting Reflex**: When you stroke the baby's cheek or the corner of their mouth, they will turn their head toward the touch, seeking the breast or bottle.
- **Mouthing and Lip Smacking**: Babies may start mouthing or smacking their lips when they are hungry to politely ask for some milk.
- **Sucking on Fingers or Hands**: Babies often bring their hands to their mouths and suck on their fingers or fists when they are hungry. Fun fact, they start doing this in the womb because it helps them swallow!

- **Crying**: This is a late hunger cue. By the time a baby is crying for food, they are quite hungry. It's best to respond to hunger cues before crying occurs.
- **Restlessness and Fidgeting**: An infant may become more active, fidgety, or exhibit restless movements when they are hungry.
- **Increased Alertness**: Hunger can make a baby more alert, with wide eyes and an attentive gaze.
- **Nuzzling at the Chest**: If held close to the breast, a hungry baby may nuzzle at the chest. Doesn't matter who is holding them!
- **Making Sucking Sounds**: Babies might make sucking sounds when they are hungry, even if they are not sucking on anything (*Understanding Your Baby's Cues*, n.d.).

Diapering and Hygiene

Let's talk diaper duty—it's a rite of passage! We were a little nervous about this part, but it's not a big deal. Mastering the changing of the diaper happened after the first few times – you got this. Creating a diapering routine will keep your little one fresh and comfy. Now, there's a whole world of diaper options out there, from disposable to natural to cloth. Your baby will likely start in the newborn size, but sometimes they jump straight to size 1 if they're on the bigger side. Just so you know, those first couple of meconium poops are like sticky, tar-like little surprises, but they'll turn yellow and seedy as things normalize.

Here's a tip: Turn it into a little competition—see how fast you can change a diaper! It's all about speed and precision. And hey, embrace the diaper duty with enthusiasm; it's part of the dad journey (*The New Dad's Survival Guide*, 2018). You'll be amazed at how much you and your partner start talking about your kid's poop!

Your Baby's Feeding and Sleep Rhythms

The first six weeks are mostly just survival, but as your baby starts growing that first month rolls by. Here's a sneak peek into what's coming your way:

Practice Patience

Your baby is going to start getting into a bit of a rhythm when it comes to feeding and sleep. But remember, it's like a little dance with unpredictable steps. So, the first lesson: is patience. These little ones have schedules that only they understand, and you're going to have to adapt and navigate some challenges along the way. Be kind to yourself and your partner during this learning curve—you're all in it together.

Naptime

And let's talk naptime—that's where you might become a Naptime Hero. This is when you get creative to ensure a peaceful nap for your little one. It's all about finding those sweet spots that make them doze off like a champ.

Just like when they are hungry, babies give various cues to signal that they are feeling sleepy or tired. Here are some common signs that your baby may be ready for a nap or bedtime:

- **Yawning**: Frequent yawning is a classic indicator of sleepiness in both babies and adults!
- **Eye Rubbing**: Babies often rub their eyes when they are tired. You might notice them vigorously rubbing their eyes or even their face.
- **Crankiness**: Increased fussiness, particularly when unrelated to hunger, discomfort, or a diaper change, may indicate that your baby is tired and in need of sleep.
- **Decreased Activity**: A tired baby may become less active, with reduced limb movements and a calmer demeanor.
- **Glazed Stare**: Your baby might have a glazed or distant look in their eyes when they are sleepy.
- **Quietness**: If your usually vocal baby becomes unusually quiet, it could be a sign of fatigue.
- **Losing Interest**: If your baby loses interest in toys or other stimuli, it might indicate sleepiness.
- **Seeking Comfort**: Your baby may become more clingy or seek comfort from a pacifier, thumb, or by being held when they are tired (*Understanding Your Baby's Cues*, n.d.).

Bathing

Learn the art of giving your baby a soothing bath, and keep in mind that it's not just about cleanliness; it's also a precious moment for bonding and sensory exploration. Typically, the first bath takes place in the sink or a small baby bathtub to ensure safety. Always remember, never leave your little one near water unsupervised, not even for a moment. Some parents prefer to wait until the umbilical cord has completely fallen off before giving that first bath. Whichever approach you choose, be extra vigilant in keeping the umbilical area clean and dry for your baby's comfort and well-being.

Comfort and Soothing

Soothing techniques, like swaddling, rocking, and shushing, are the magic tricks in your parenting toolkit for keeping your little one happy and content. They provide a sense of comfort and serenity, helping your baby feel safe and snug. Usually, this works by mimicking the environment they experienced in the womb.

- **Swaddling**: Swaddling involves wrapping your baby snugly in a blanket or cloth, leaving only their head exposed. This practice mimics the cozy feeling of being in your partner's stomach. Swaddling helps babies feel secure by restricting their movements and preventing the startle reflex. It can promote better sleep and soothe a fussy baby. However, it's crucial to swaddle safely, ensuring that your baby's hips have enough room to move and breathe.
- **Rocking**: Rocking involves gently moving your baby back and forth, usually in your arms or a baby rocker or cradle. Rocking is comforting for babies because it simulates the motion they experienced in the womb. The rhythmic movement can calm a fussy baby and help them fall asleep. However, always ensure that the rocking is gentle and controlled to prevent any discomfort or harm.

- **Shushing**: Shushing involves making a gentle shushing or white noise sound to create a soothing background noise for your baby. The shushing sound is reminiscent of the whooshing noises babies hear while in utero. It can be remarkably effective in masking other sounds and calming a baby. You can achieve this by using a white noise machine, a recording, or even simply making the sound yourself by saying "shh" repeatedly. It's a straightforward but powerful tool for settling a fussy baby.

And if you want to level up your soothing game, become a Pacifier Ninja—that means swiftly and skillfully popping a pacifier back into your baby's mouth when needed. It's like being the superhero of comfort in your baby's world!

Handling Infant Challenges and Illnesses

Handling infant challenges and illnesses is an essential part of parenthood. Babies may encounter common issues such as teething and colic. It's crucial to recognize signs of illness and know when to seek medical advice. When your little one isn't feeling their best, providing comfort and care is your top priority. To navigate these challenges effectively, educate yourself about these issues and maintain open communication with your partner on how to alleviate your baby's discomfort. Trust your parental instincts, but don't hesitate to seek professional guidance from healthcare professionals when necessary. Keep baby Tylenol on hand just in case!

Every one of these conditions comes with its own set of difficulties and potential treatments (*Common Health Problems and Diseases in Babies*, 2021):

Colic

Colic is characterized by intense crying lasting at least three hours and occurring more than three times a week in infants aged two weeks to four months. The cause of colic is not fully understood, but it may relate to an upset belly. Intervention strategies include dietary changes and providing gentle back pats during crying episodes. Additional techniques involve feeding the baby slowly while lying down and using cool clothing on hot days for soothing. Don't overlook remedies such as baby leg exercises and gripe water!

Cold and Flu

Kids are more susceptible to colds and flu due to their less mature immune systems. Vaccination and over-the-counter medications for fever or pain relief are options for keeping them healthy. Pediatricians recommend vaccinating when necessary and providing over-the-counter medications to manage symptoms. We highly recommend a good humidifier to have bedside for this! And once they are 3 months and beyond, keep a chest and foot rub on hand to help open airways!

Ear Infections

Ear infections are prevalent among children, often requiring biannual checkups. They occur when fluid accumulates behind the eardrum, leading to pain, redness, fever, and varying symptoms based on the type of infection. Treatment may involve antibiotics depending on severity, and pediatricians offer guidance to prevent future episodes.

Baby Acne

Baby acne can occur in infants aged three to six months and primarily affects the cheeks and forehead. Pediatricians may prescribe over-the-counter medications like benzoyl peroxide as needed.

Bacterial Conjunctivitis

Bacterial conjunctivitis (aka pink eye) manifests as redness, watery eyes, and discharge from one or both eyes. It may result from bacteria introduced through dirty hands, objects, contact with infected individuals, or excessive exposure to bright light.

Diaper Rash

Diaper rash results from prolonged contact with urine and/or stool in the diaper area and can be triggered by insufficient air circulation, diaper or wipe sensitivity, or food allergies. Pediatricians may recommend topical ointments like zinc oxide for this condition.

Tonsillitis

Tonsillitis occurs when the tonsils become swollen and inflamed due to bacterial infection, typically Streptococcus pneumonia. In cases of recurrent infections unresponsive to antibiotics, tonsillectomy surgery may be necessary.

Jaundice

Jaundice causes a yellowish discoloration of the skin, eyes, and/or whites of the eyes. It can result from an immature liver in newborns or inadequate breastfeeding, leading to bilirubin buildup in the blood.

SLEEP DEPRIVATION AND SELF-CARE

Sleep Strategies

The reality of sleepless nights can be daunting, but you're not alone. Look into strategies like taking turns with nighttime feedings and naps. Sharing the load helps both of you get some much-needed rest. Plus, remember, it's like learning a new language; you'll figure out what works best for your baby. "Sleep when the baby sleeps" is a common piece of advice given to new parents, and it's all about prioritizing your own rest during the early months of parenthood. When your baby takes a nap, you should use that time to rest or sleep as well, especially if you're feeling tired or sleep-deprived. Here are a few additional suggestions to help new dads get better sleep:

- Be Sleep-Ready: Keep an eye mask, water, earplugs, and comfy pillows and blankets within reach to seize any sleep opportunity.
- Skip Alcohol: Avoid alcohol close to bedtime, as it disrupts sleep; opt for non-caffeinated drinks to stay hydrated.
- Stock Up: Keep the changing table well-supplied with diapers for quick nighttime changes, reducing the need for late-night calls for help.
- Early to Bed: Resist the Netflix temptation and head to bed early to prepare for unpredictable nighttime awakenings; avoid screens and try relaxation techniques for easier sleep.
- Eat Right: Have a healthy lunch if you're back at work, avoiding heavy meals to prevent afternoon drowsiness and improve sleep quality.
- Take Turns: Sleep on the sofa or in a spare room a few nights during the week if possible to assist with nighttime duties, and trade-off with your partner on weekends for uninterrupted rest (McGinn, 2019).

The Reality of Sleepless Nights

Surviving the exhausting reality of sleepless nights as a new parent involves understanding and dealing with the challenges of sleep deprivation. During these trying times, consider using gentle touch as a soothing technique for your baby. Experiment with methods we discussed like rocking, swaddling, and gentle pats to figure out what works best to provide comfort and reassurance. Babywearing can be a valuable tool, allowing you to keep your baby close while having the freedom to move around hands-free. You might hear the term "dadnesia," which is the dad version of "baby brain." It's all the forgetfulness caused by lack of sleep and the demands of parenting. Embrace it with humor; it's a rite of passage. "Dad Fuel," can be your trusted coffee or other caffeinated beverages (or something stronger on the really hard days).

Now, when it comes to managing your baby's unpredictable schedule, it's a good idea to create a routine when you can. When I discuss a sleep schedule for a one-month-old, keep in mind the motto of a "flexible routine, not a rigid schedule" (Dumaplin, 2023a). This will help your baby get used to sleeping at certain times, and it can make a huge difference in helping them sleep through the night.

Another important tip is to take turns with your partner when it comes to handling nighttime feedings. And here's a big one: Set up a schedule between you and your partner before the baby arrives. Knowing who's going to take care of the baby during the night is a game-changer. And if your wife plans on breastfeeding exclusively, suggest she pumps some milk, so you can take a nighttime shift and give baby a bottle. Remember, a well-rested mom is better equipped to care for your baby, so teamwork is crucial during these challenging times. The sleepless nights won't last forever.

Self-Care

With all the baby's demands, don't forget about self-care. Find time to relax, read, exercise, or just take a deep breath. It's vital for your well-being, and a happier you means a happier family. Self-care for new dads is all about maintaining your physical and emotional well-being while dealing with the demands of parenthood.

Taking care of yourself as a new dad involves several important aspects. First and foremost, maintaining a balanced diet is crucial. Eating well not only keeps you healthy but also provides the energy you need to keep up with your baby's needs and your daily responsibilities. Additionally, incorporating regular physical activity into your routine, such as short work-outs or walks, can help you stay active and relieve stress, improving your overall well-being.

Equally important is your mental health. Pay close attention to it and don't hesitate to seek professional help or talk to a therapist if you're feeling overwhelmed, anxious, or experiencing postpartum depression.

Stay connected with friends and family. Isolation can be a common issue for new parents, so maintaining social connections can provide much-needed support and offer valuable perspective during this transformative phase of life.

Asking for Help

Don't hesitate to ask for help. Share parenting duties with your partner, ask family or friends to assist when needed, or consider hiring a babysitter for a break. Remember that asking for help is a sign of strength, not weakness.

STRENGTHENING YOUR RELATIONSHIP

The early phases of entering parenthood can indeed throw some challenges your way as you figure out how to care for your new baby. But this can also be an incredible opportunity for you and your partner to grow and strengthen your relationship. The key is to be intentional. Talk openly with each other, learn what each of you needs, and find ways to support one another. By doing this, you'll build a solid foundation for your parenting journey and create a deeper connection as you tackle the ups and downs of raising your child together.

Open Communication

Maintaining a strong and healthy relationship as parents starts with one fundamental thing: communication. It's not just about talking but listening and understanding each other. Share your feelings, experiences, and challenges openly. This kind of open dialogue is your best defense against misunderstandings. Make it a habit to have ongoing conversations and check-ins. That way, you both feel heard, understood, and supported.

Shared Responsibilities

It's all about teamwork when it comes to maintaining that healthy balance and avoiding feeling overwhelmed as parents. You and your partner should share the responsibilities and parenting duties (Taylor, 2022). This includes tasks like diaper changes, feeding, and soothing your baby. When you work together and divide the workload, you're not only establishing a sense of teamwork but also giving both of you the chance to bond with your baby. Teamwork creates a strong support system and fosters a loving and nurturing environment for your child to grow and thrive in.

Date Nights

Parenting is undoubtedly demanding, but don't forget to set aside time for each other. Despite the challenges that come with raising a child, it's vital to keep your relationship a priority and nurture that special connection. It could be as straightforward as scheduling regular date nights or ensuring you spend quality time together. I get it, leaving your baby might seem tough at first, but it's a hurdle worth overcoming. If you don't, you might end up feeling isolated and detached from the world outside your home. You don't want to be the parents who haven't left the house in 3 years.

Empathy

Being empathetic toward your partner is all about understanding and sharing their feelings and experiences as you both tackle parenthood. It's like stepping into their shoes and acknowledging their emotions, needs, and challenges without judgment. Why is this important? Well, parenthood can throw a lot at you.

By practicing empathy, you create a nurturing space within your relationship. It means being there for your partner when they're struggling—whether it's dealing with the relentless lack of sleep, adapting to new parenting responsibilities, or navigating the emotional highs and lows that come with raising a child. Show them understanding, offer comfort, and provide encouragement. This not only makes them feel heard, validated, and less isolated, but it also strengthens your bond and improves communication between you two.

EMBRACING THE JOURNEY

We've been on this wild parenting journey, and remember this: The newborn phase, as intense as it may seem right now, is just a blink in the grand scheme of things. It's a challenging period, but it's also a unique chance for personal growth and strengthening your relationship with your partner.

During the sleepless nights and endless diaper changes, there are these extraordinary moments that'll warm your heart. Think of your baby's first real smile—it's like a ray of sunshine on the gloomiest day. Those moments are the small victories you'll treasure as your child grows. They're your reminder of the sheer joy of being a parent.

Now, let's talk about those times when you're both feeling overwhelmed and exhausted. Trust me, it happens to the best of us. That's when your partner transforms into your greatest ally, your confidant, and your trusty teammate. These challenges may seem insurmountable, but they're also the glue that binds you even closer. When you face them together, your connection deepens, and you'll emerge from this phase with a nearly indestructible bond.

So, my fellow parent, embrace this journey with an open heart. It's a rollercoaster ride, no doubt, but it's filled with love, laughter, and precious memories waiting for you along the way. Savor every moment, relish the small wins, and lean on each other for strength and support.

DAD'S WORKOUT

- Gear up for the baby rodeo, Dad! Master the art of feeding (bonus points if you don't end up wearing more formula than the baby), diapering like a pro (consider it a speed challenge), and bathing—think of it as a splashy adventure with a tiny co-pilot. And don't forget about taking care of yourself—sleep deprivation is a battle, but you can handle it like a drowsy but determined ninja. You may have to up your caffeine intake, but it's a small sacrifice for the greatness of being a parent.

- Maintaining a strong relationship is important, even if it means deciphering tired grunts and communicating amidst the chaos. Share responsibilities with your partner like a well-coordinated dance—extra points if you can change a diaper together without waking the baby. And in the craziness, find those precious moments of quality time. It may involve reheating your coffee multiple times, but it's worth it for those bonding rituals.
- So, embrace the mess, the giggles, and the sleepless nights—it's not insanity, it's the epic saga of growing and connecting as a family. Dad life: where every challenge is a chance to level up!

CHAPTER 7
THE JOURNEY CONTINUES: NAVIGATING THE FIRST MONTHS OF PARENTHOOD

 Life doesn't come with an instruction book—that's why we have fathers.

H. JACKSON BROWNE

You've now survived the delivery and very early stages with your newborn – whatever nerdy celebratory gesture you want to make, now's the time – get those fist pumps and air guitar ready! However, you still have a long way to go, and we're here to help. We'll give some helpful insights into your journey through those initial months with your newborn after the newborn phase.

Let's start with routines. Babies may not be able to articulate it, but they thrive on structure. Creating a predictable routine is not only comforting for your little one but also a game-changer for you. We'll discuss wake windows, essentially how long your baby can stay awake at different ages. Then, onto the essentials: timing meals, making playtime engaging, and creating a peaceful environment for naps.

But parenting is about more than just schedules. It's about building strong bonds and shaping your baby's development. Your consistent presence matters more than you might realize. We'll explore how your everyday caregiving routines, like changing diapers and feeding, build trust and attachment. And let's not forget the importance of play. Playtime isn't just about fun; it's a crucial tool for your baby's cognitive and emotional development. You'll also find age-appropriate activities to engage and challenge your little one.

As we wrap up, we'll celebrate the milestones you and your baby achieve together, from their first smile to your growing ability to soothe them. These milestones are building blocks for your child's future. Parenthood may not come with an instruction manual, but with the right knowledge and a few laughs, we'll navigate it just fine.

ESTABLISH ROUTINES

Listen, as your little one grows, you'll find that sticking to a daily routine is providing them with a sense of stability and security. This part of the journey is all about helping you create a daily rhythm that caters to your baby's changing needs and ensures they feel safe and cared for.

Understanding Your Baby's Patterns

Babies, like adults, have unique patterns and preferences. By paying attention to your baby's natural rhythms for feeding, sleeping, and play, you can tailor your daily routine to align with your baby's individual patterns. For instance, if your baby tends to get sleepy at a particular time, you can schedule naptime accordingly. This approach ensures that your baby feels comfortable and cared for because their routine is in sync with their natural inclinations.

Flexibility and Adaptability

While consistency in a routine is essential, babies are known for their growth spurts, developmental changes, and the occasional unexpected situation. It's important to remain flexible and adaptable in your routine. This flexibility allows you to accommodate your baby's changing needs, ensuring they continue to feel secure even as they grow and develop. For example, you might need to adjust feeding times as your baby's appetite changes during growth spurts (Masters, 2021).

Predictable Transitions

Creating smooth transitions between activities is another key component of establishing routines. Predictable transitions involve helping your baby move seamlessly from one activity to another, such as transitioning from playtime to naptime. Predictability in these transitions is essential because it helps your baby anticipate what comes next, reducing their anxiety (Thistel, 2022). For instance, if you have a set routine of calming activities before naptime, your baby learns to associate those cues with sleep, making the transition smoother and less stressful for them.

BALANCING MEALTIME, PLAYTIME, AND NAPTIME

Strategically Timing Meals

When it comes to feeding your baby, pay attention to their cues. Babies have a way of letting you know when they're hungry. Look for signs like rooting or sucking on their fists. By aligning feeding with these cues, you're responding to their needs promptly. So, plan your feeding times around these hunger signals. Also, make mealtime a quiet and comfy affair. This sets the stage for a positive and relaxed feeding experience.

Engaging Playtime

Playtime isn't just about keeping your little one entertained; it's about helping them grow and learn. So, get playful! Use toys that make them curious, play with different textures, and create an interactive environment that stimulates their senses and cognitive development. Think of it as learning through play. It's not only fun but also a great way to nurture their young minds.

Nurturing Naptime

You can establish a schedule for your baby, even if they are very young, by considering their "nap gap" (Johnson, 2023). Also called a "wake window", this refers to the length of time between sleep periods, including the time between naps and between their final nap and bedtime. Establishing a peaceful naptime routine is essential for helping your baby transition to sleep. We recommend creating an environment that signals wind-down time and is the same, time after time. This might involve dimming the lights and setting a calming atmosphere. Using soothing techniques, such as gentle rocking or a lullaby, can help your baby relax and prepare for naptime. The goal is to make the transition to sleep as smooth and soothing as possible, ensuring your baby gets the rest they need.

BUILDING LASTING BONDS AND SHAPING DEVELOPMENT

Developing a Strong Parent-Child Bond Through Consistent Care

Your role as a parent is not just about meeting your baby's physical needs; it's also about nurturing their emotional and cognitive development. This begins with consistent care. It involves being there for your baby consistently and responding to their needs promptly and with sensitivity. Your reliable presence is like a reassuring anchor in your baby's world, building a profound sense of security and trust.

Reliable Presence

Being consistently present and responsive to your baby's needs is a cornerstone of building a strong parent-child bond. When your baby knows they can count on you to meet their needs, it fosters a sense of security and trust. This consistency in your caregiving, from feeding to comforting moments, sends a powerful message to your baby that you're there for them, no matter what. Your reliable presence is like a rock that your baby can lean on, promoting emotional well-being and attachment. When they cry or need something, and you're there like clockwork, it tells them, "Hey, I've got your back."

Attachment Building

Around the age of three months, your baby's social instincts start to shine. They'll seek out interactions with you and other significant caregivers, making a real effort to keep these connections going (*Development of Attachment*, 2023). Gradually, their attention will shift more toward you and other familiar faces. Plus, they'll become quite the expert at turning their head and focusing on your familiar voice. Engaging in caregiving routines with sensitivity and warmth is key to forming a strong attachment with your baby. Changing diapers, feeding, and comforting moments are not just practical tasks; they are opportunities for emotional connection. This bond is nurtured through your dad gaze, those moments when you lovingly watch your baby play or achieve milestones. Remember, bonding can take time, and that's normal. Some dads take up to six months to fully bond with their newborns, so be patient with the process (Corner & Chan, 2018).

THE ROLE OF PLAY IN COGNITIVE AND EMOTIONAL DEVELOPMENT

Learning Through Play

Playtime isn't just for fun; it's a powerful tool for your baby's brain development. It helps them learn problem-solving skills and explore their senses. Participating in interactive play is crucial for the development of your baby. When you actively engage in playtime, you provide valuable information that helps your baby understand the world around them. Even something as simple as a game of peekaboo can teach them that things that disappear can reappear—a big "aha" moment for them (*Thinking and Play*, 2018).

Emotional Expression

Engaging in play is an essential aspect of your baby's development, as it offers a secure environment for them to express their emotions, understand the concept of cause and effect, and begin to cultivate a sense of control over their actions. Playtime isn't just about games; it's a playground for emotional expression, a laboratory of understanding, and a launching pad for self-discovery. Through imaginative and pretend play, children often recreate real-life scenarios, which allows them to act out and make sense of their emotions in a controlled setting. For example, when they are toddlers, they might have dolls or action figures engage in conversations or conflicts that mirror their own experiences. So, as you watch your baby play, know that every smile, every laugh, and every discovery is a step in their incredible journey of growth.

Engaging in Interactive Activities to Stimulate Growth

Age-Appropriate Activities

Choose play activities that match your baby's developmental stage. From tummy time to stacking blocks, these activities challenge and engage your baby. Engaging activities for newborns play a crucial role in their early development by fostering sensory awareness, muscle use, and emotional connections.

- **Side-Lying Neck Stretch**: Place your baby on their side beneath a mobile, about 8 to 12 inches away. Gently spin the mobile to encourage them to stretch their neck muscles. Alternate sides to ensure balanced development.
- **Stimulate With Tactile Play**: Use items like a baby washcloth, silky scarf, or a mitten to gently stroke your baby's feet, hands, belly, and face. This tactile

stimulation enhances body awareness and strengthens your bond.

- **Exploring Temperature**: Introduce your baby to temperature differences by dipping cotton balls in cool and warm water, then gently brushing them. This sensory experience helps your baby recognize different sensations on their skin.

- **Tummy Time from the Start**: Start tummy time early, using black-and-white images placed within your baby's line of sight (8 to 12 inches away). Placing your newborn across your legs stimulates their eyesight, engagement, and body strengthening.

- **A Calming Massage**: Massaging your baby promotes relaxation and sleep. Lay your baby on a soft surface, use a gentle smoothing motion to massage their body, and continue until your child indicates they've had enough or falls asleep.

- **Focus Play**: Use a black-and-white rattle or small toy, holding it 8 to 12 inches away from your baby. Wait for them to focus on it, then slowly turn the toy to develop their visual skills.

- **Read Together**: Reading to your newborn, despite their limited understanding, introduces them to the joy of reading and strengthens your emotional connection. Your voice and scent provide comfort, allowing them to observe and explore their new world (*7 Engaging Activities for Newborns*, 2022).

Quality Over Quantity

During playtime, focus on the quality of interactions. Engage in eye contact, respond to your baby's cues, and follow their lead to create a meaningful experience. High-quality interactions in early childhood involve several key features that focus on creating a warm, responsive, and engaging environment for children's social and emotional development, language acquisition, and cognitive growth.

- **Attuned and Responsive Adults**: The role of the adult is to be attuned to children's needs and responsive to their cues. This involves establishing trusting and warm relationships with young children. Adults should attend to children's social and emotional well-being and development, as this has a positive impact on language development.
- **Maintain Eye Contact**: When engaging in conversation with children, adults should maintain eye contact. This simple action helps set the stage for communication and shows that the adult is attentive and interested.
- **Warm and Receptive Attitude**: Adults should welcome and encourage children's attempts to communicate. A warm and receptive attitude fosters an environment where children feel safe to express themselves.
- **Promote Friendship and Cooperation**: Encouraging children's friendship skills, emotional understanding, and expression is essential. Adults should offer opportunities for children to practice these skills, such as sharing, through cooperative games, and by valuing positive behaviors.
- **Listening and Back-and-Forth Conversations**: The role of the adult is to listen actively to children and encourage sustained back-and-forth conversations. This "serve and return" interaction pattern provides children with a blueprint for turn-taking in conversations.
- **Join in With Children's Play**: Adults can sensitively join in with children's play by following their lead and focusing on the child's interests. This shared attention

helps build rapport and provides opportunities for meaningful conversation.

- **Scaffold Language Responsively**: Adults should listen carefully to what children say and respond by expanding and extending their language. This approach helps enrich children's vocabulary and language skills.
- **Model Talking About What Children See and Do**: Instead of constantly asking questions, adults should describe and comment on what children see and do. This approach helps children connect language to their experiences.
- **Engage in Back-and-Forth Conversations**: High-quality interactions involve conversations that have multiple turns. Adults should aim to involve children in more than four conversational turns, which provides ample opportunities for language development.
- **Make It Meaningful**: Utilize everyday routines and activities, such as snack time, as social opportunities. These moments offer a rich context for conversation and relationship-building.
- **Go Beyond the "Here and Now"**: As children grow, it's important to start using "decontextualized talk" to broaden their understanding of word meanings. Engage in pretend play, discuss past and future events, offer explanations, and encourage conversations that expand children's knowledge and language skills.
- **Wait**: Always give children time to listen, process, and respond. Patience is key in ensuring that children feel heard and valued in the interaction (James, 2022).

Parent-Child Interaction

Actively participating during playtime strengthens your bond with your baby, fostering a secure attachment. Making eye contact is a powerful form of communication that assures your baby of your undivided attention, enhancing trust and a sense of security. Additionally, physical touch, like holding, cuddling, or gently stroking your baby's fingers and toes during playtime, reinforces your love and care, offering comfort and safety. Engaging in shared exploration together is like embarking on a journey to discover the world. This can involve playing with toys, examining objects, or exploring their surroundings, all contributing to your baby's learning and growth.

Emotional Foundation

Play serves as an emotional foundation for your baby's development. During the early months, your emotional availability plays a crucial role in shaping your baby's emotional intelligence. As you engage in play and interactions with your little one, they learn to trust their own emotions and begin to develop healthy coping strategies.

Positive Experiences

During playtime, it's important to create a safe and loving environment for your baby. This environment allows your little one to freely explore and express themselves without fear or apprehension. These positive and nurturing experiences during play

lay the foundation for a confident and emotionally secure future.

Nurturing Your Baby's Early Social and Cognitive Growth

Encouraging Interaction

Encouraging social interaction is a fundamental component of your baby's development. It offers opportunities for them to learn valuable skills such as communication, sharing, and empathy. By fostering these interactions, you provide your baby with a strong foundation for social and cognitive growth.

These early social experiences not only help your baby develop critical social skills but also enhance their cognitive abilities. As they engage in communication and interaction with family members and peers, their language skills improve, and their understanding of the world deepens.

Stimulating Cognitive Exploration

Introduce new textures, shapes, and sounds to stimulate cognitive growth. Your baby's brain forms connections through these sensory experiences. Toys play a vital role in stimulating cognitive development in children. These toys encourage flexible thinking, experimentation, imitation, and problem-solving, all of which are fundamental aspects of cognitive growth.

- **Building and Construction Toys**: Toys like blocks and connecting sets are great for promoting cognitive development. They are considered "open-ended" toys, allowing children to create structures in different ways. This type of play helps children develop skills such as paying attention to how things fit together, controlling their impulses to prevent their creations from falling down, and thinking flexibly by trying out different configurations. It also encourages children to think creatively and come up with new ideas each time they play.

- **Pretend Play Toys**: These toys support cognitive development in multiple ways. Children can choose different roles, act out various situations, and interact with props and costumes. Pretend play stimulates their memory for events and activities, as they often re-enact real-life situations. It also helps them practice sequencing, where they put actions together to create a storyline.

- **Puzzles and Open-Ended Fine Motor Toys**: Puzzles and fine motor toys promote cognitive exploration by requiring children to observe and fit pieces into the correct spots. These activities help children understand concepts like geometric shapes and sizes and give teachers opportunities to model problem-solving strategies. They also encourage discussions about patterns and other math-related topics.

- **Cause and Effect Toys**: These toys are designed to teach children about cause and effect. They usually involve actions like pushing buttons, sliding sliders, or turning handles to create a specific result. These toys enhance children's understanding of the relationship between actions and outcomes and help develop their fine motor skills.

- **Sensory Exploration Toys and Materials**: Sensory play is a fundamental aspect of cognitive development. It allows children to explore different textures and substances safely. These activities could consist of simple setups like tubs filled with sand or rice for tactile exploration. Sensory play with water, bubbles, or various materials provides opportunities for children to engage their senses and learn through hands-on experiences.

- **Household Items and Natural Materials**: Everyday objects found around the house and natural materials from the outdoors offer valuable opportunities for children to observe, categorize, and discover the world around them. These items can be used in various ways to encourage exploration and foster cognitive development (*Toys and Materials That Support Cognitive Development*, 2020).

Marking and Celebrating Milestones

Take joy in celebrating every milestone your baby reaches during their early development journey. For instance, when your baby greets you with their first smile, it's a moment of pure delight and a significant social milestone. This smile represents their growing connection and recognition of your presence, and it's a testament to the trust and security they feel in your care.

Likewise, becoming proficient at diapering may seem mundane, but it's a skill that ensures your baby's comfort and hygiene. Mastering this task showcases your commitment and caregiving prowess.

Comforting your baby with a gentle touch, soothing words, or your loving embrace is another remarkable milestone. It signifies your ability to understand your baby's needs and provide the warmth and reassurance they seek.

Importance of Milestones

Developmental milestones are key markers that indicate your baby's growth and progress across various areas of development, including physical, cognitive, social, and emotional domains.

As your baby reaches the age of one month, they are starting to adjust to their surroundings and routine. At this stage, there are several developmental milestones you can expect to see (*Well-Baby Care Visits & Developmental Milestones*, n.d.):

- Your baby will begin to raise their hands up to their face.
- They will also start moving their head from side to side.
- They will start to grasp their fists tightly.
- They will become more alert and aware of the sounds around them.
- Your baby will begin to recognize faces.
- In terms of feeding, you can expect them to consume formula or breastmilk every three to four hours.

During 2 to 3 months, your baby will continue to refine their motor skills as they gain a better understanding of how their body operates. Some important milestones for your growing baby include:

- Progressing in their ability to lift their head and chest off the ground while on their stomach.
- Beginning to vocalize with cooing and gurgling sounds.

- Relaxing their clenched fists and demonstrating the ability to reach for and grasp objects.
- Tracking moving objects with their eyes and showing more focus and attention.
- Smiling at people, particularly their primary caregivers, as they become more social and interactive.

Tracking Progress

Developmental milestones provide a framework for tracking your baby's development. They offer a way to measure and ensure that your child is progressing in a healthy and expected manner. If your baby is consistently meeting these milestones, it's a positive sign that they are on the right developmental track.

On the other hand, if your baby is consistently not reaching specific milestones within the expected timeframe, it could be an early indicator of a developmental delay or issue. Identifying such concerns early allows for timely intervention and support, which can be crucial in addressing potential challenges and helping your child catch up.

Fostering a Strong Bond

Take a moment to think about those tender moments you've shared, like when your baby gave you their first heartwarming smile or the times you comforted them in your arms. These are the building blocks of a strong connection that will last a lifetime. Celebrate this unique bond between you and your baby.

It's something truly special, and it's going to continue growing as your baby does.

Looking Forward

As you look back on the incredible journey you've started with your baby, also keep your eyes on the future. There are so many exciting adventures ahead, and your role as a father will keep evolving. From those first steps to the first words, your presence and guidance will be instrumental in shaping your child's life. The bond you've cultivated will only deepen as your baby grows, and you'll discover new aspects of your relationship. Embrace the journey with open arms and a loving heart, and enjoy every moment because, believe me, it goes by faster than you can imagine.

DAD'S WORKOUT

- Understand your baby's patterns and be adaptable in your routine to cater to their changing needs.
- When it comes to meals, engage in responsive feeding, setting the stage for a positive and relaxed experience.
- Playtime is more than fun; it's a powerful tool for cognitive and emotional development. Your role in playtime is like a guide on their fascinating journey.

CHAPTER 8
EXPLORING THE WORLD: BABY ON THE MOVE

(HALF A YEAR OF GROWTH: CELEBRATING BABY'S 6-MONTH MARK)

 Every son's first superhero is his father.

TIGER SHROFF

Becoming a parent is a transformative journey, and as your baby continues to grow, each moment is filled with new experiences and milestones. In this chapter, we'll explore the exciting world of a mobile baby, discovering the joys and challenges that come with their newfound mobility. From those first adorable rolls and sits to the exploration of tastes and textures through solid foods, there's a whole universe to uncover. We'll guide introducing solids, surviving the teething phase, and nurturing your baby's communication and language development. As your little one begins to crawl and explore, we'll offer valuable insights on creating a safe and stimulating environment for their adventures, both inside and outside your home. So, fasten your seatbelt, because this chapter is all about embracing the world of a baby on the move – and don't worry, it won't just be baby on the move – you gotta keep up!

MOTOR MILESTONES: ROLLING, SITTING, AND MORE

As your baby reaches the age of exploration, they begin hitting significant motor milestones. These include those precious moments when they first learn to roll over or sit up. Watching these achievements is like witnessing your child unfold a new chapter of independence. It's essential to encourage these developments by providing a safe and supportive environment for them to practice and perfect their newfound skills.

Grasping and Manipulating Objects

During this stage, your little one's tiny hands are developing their own set of skills. They'll amaze you with their ability to grasp and manipulate objects, signaling their curiosity about the world around them. Engaging with toys that stimulate their tactile senses will not only enhance their motor skills but also foster their cognitive growth.

Visual and Auditory Development

Your baby's world is continually expanding, and their sense of sight and sound plays a vital role in their early development. By responding to your baby's visual and auditory cues, you help them build the foundation for communication and understanding. Encourage their visual and auditory exploration by introducing them to colorful and engaging stimuli that capture their attention and stimulate their senses. And feel free to get weird here – as in, speak baby back to them – not real words but more the process of responding to them as if you were having a baby-talk conversation.

By the time six months have passed, the baby's depth perception will have greatly improved. They will now be capable of seeing things that are located at a greater distance, potentially reaching several feet or more. Moreover, they will be able to concentrate on objects without their eyes crossing and will also be able to discern between different colors.

Introducing Solid Foods

Around six months, you'll embark on an exciting journey as you introduce solid foods to your baby's diet (*6-Month-Old Baby*, 2019). This marks the beginning of their culinary adventure, and it's a thrilling time for both you and your child. It's important to approach this stage with patience, as your baby explores new tastes and textures. Start with simple, age-appropriate purees that allow them to experience different sensations through self-feeding, even if it results in a bit of mess.

Solid Starts is a website and online resource dedicated to helping parents and caregivers introduce solid foods to their babies and support them on their journey of transitioning from breast milk or formula to a more diverse diet. The website offers a wealth of information, guidance, and tools related to baby nutrition, including expert advice, recipes, articles, videos, and other resources. They also have a database that indicates when a food can be introduced.

FEEDING AND NUTRITION: INTRODUCING SOLID FOODS

Starting Solids: When and How

Knowing when to start introducing solid foods to your baby and how to do it properly is important. One way to determine if a food is suitable for your baby is by using the "finger test." This means that the food should be soft and easily squishable when you press it between your fingers.

If your baby can sit up and support their head, that is an excellent initial indication they are ready. Furthermore, if they bring objects to their mouth and display curiosity about what you are eating, it may indicate that your inquisitive little one is ready to begin consuming solid foods.

Another important aspect of starting solids is allowing babies to play with their food. While it may seem messy, it's a valuable part of their development. Allowing babies to touch, feel, and explore different textures and tastes can stimulate their senses and help them become more comfortable with solid foods. It's a great way to encourage self-feeding and the development of fine motor skills.

Best First Foods

When babies turn 6 months old, they often start exploring their chewing abilities. They may not have fully mastered this skill yet, but they are usually excited to try out messy and soft pureed foods. Introducing solids at this stage is not meant to replace their liquid diet, but rather to arouse their curiosity and interest in different flavors and textures.

Because infants grow rapidly, their need for iron is significant. Introduce iron-rich foods such as infant cereals, well-cooked meats, mashed beans, and lentils into their diet. Here is a list of great first foods to introduce to your baby:

- Infant oats, grain, or barley cereals mixed with breastmilk or formula, can be spoon-fed to your baby.
- Sweet potato puree, offers a delightful taste and smooth texture.
- Squash puree provides a mild and easy-to-digest option.
- Pea puree, which is both nutritious and gentle on a baby's stomach.
- Carrot puree, is packed with vitamins and a naturally sweet flavor.
- Mashed banana, offers a creamy consistency and familiar taste.
- Mashed avocado, is known for its healthy fats and creamy texture.
- Mashed or pureed beans are a great source of protein and fiber.
- Mashed or pureed lentils are another excellent protein and fiber source.
- Pureed meats such as beef, chicken, or turkey, provide essential nutrients for growth.

- Soft, tender meats like salmon, beef, chicken, or turkey that easily break apart to ensure safe consumption (*The Best First Foods for Babies*, n.d.).

TEETHING

The arrival of your baby's first teeth is an unforgettable milestone, but it often comes with its share of challenges. Teething is associated with increased drooling, runny noses, and occasionally mild fevers. Don't freak out; these are common signs as your baby's teeth emerge. To ease their discomfort, consider using baby Tylenol or frozen teething sticks. Always ensure you follow recommended dosages and safety guidelines as your baby explores this new phase of growth.

NAVIGATING ALLERGIES AND SENSITIVITIES

As you introduce a variety of foods to your baby, it's essential to be aware of potential allergies and sensitivities. Every child is different, and some may react to certain foods. Staying informed about common food allergens and paying close attention to your baby's reactions can help you identify and manage potential issues. Should you encounter any concerns, seek guidance from healthcare professionals to ensure your baby's well-being.

If you suspect your baby might have food allergies, don't panic. Many infants go through this, and it's more common than you might think. The most common allergens are often referred to as the "Big-8," including wheat, soy, fish, shellfish, eggs, cow's milk, peanuts, and tree nuts (DeMauro, 2013). Recognizing food allergies or intolerances in your little one can be tricky because their symptoms can overlap with typical baby issues. Eczema, diarrhea, constipation, and rashes—they're all part of the baby package, right? Here's where the real detective work comes in.

Testing for allergies isn't that reliable in infants, so you might have to rely on observation. Most kids eventually outgrow their allergies, and testing can be more accurate when they're a bit older. Start by keeping a food and symptoms diary, or just simply noting their reaction when fed certain foods. Look for patterns over a couple of weeks—it can be a game-changer and can help you spot the culprits. For example, our child had a mild peanut allergy when very young and got mild rashes when eating peanut-based foods; however, after eating peanut butter several times, the allergy went away and our child now loves the classic PB&J sandwich, without the rash.

CREATING HEALTHY EATING HABITS

Nurturing a positive relationship with food begins in infancy. Encouraging healthy eating habits early on can shape your baby's dietary choices in the future. By offering a balanced and nutritious diet, you lay the groundwork for a lifetime of good eating practices. Your baby learns not only about different foods but also about mealtime routines and social interactions centered around food, helping them develop a positive attitude toward eating. Eating together as a family can set a positive example. Babies often learn by watching and imitating, so seeing you enjoy a variety of foods can encourage them to do the same.

SLEEP PATTERNS AND ESTABLISHING ROUTINES

With your baby growing and exploring the world, you'll also notice changes in their sleep patterns. As they reach six months, these sleep adjustments are a natural part of their development. Establishing a bedtime routine and managing daytime naps can help ensure a restful and peaceful sleep for your little one. However, be prepared to address common sleep challenges, as each baby is unique, and their sleep habits can vary.

SLEEP CHANGES AT 6 MONTHS

Around the 6-month mark, you'll notice some sleep changes in your baby. Many babies start to transition to a more regular sleep schedule, which means longer periods of nighttime sleep. This can be a relief for tired parents! However, some babies may also experience sleep disruptions like teething or growth spurts, leading to night awakenings. It's essential to stay flexible and patient during this phase, as sleep patterns can vary from one baby to another. If your baby's sleep schedule gets a bit wonky, it's usually temporary. Keep a consistent bedtime routine, and things should settle down.

We suggest sticking to your schedule as much as possible. The discipline of retaining routine will pay off in promoting sleep. Our child experienced a sleep regression around 6 months, where one week would be much different than the next. It was very difficult to stick to a schedule and maintain sufficient sleep for us. However, we partnered together to agree on a schedule of when one parent would assume baby responsibilities and we maintained our established routine to the best of our ability. Despite a few rough weeks, the regression passed and we resumed with our normal broadcast, albeit with only slight sleep deprivation.

Creating a Bedtime Routine

Establishing a bedtime routine is a game-changer. A consistent routine signals to your baby that it's time for sleep, helping them wind down. Start with calming activities like a warm bath, gentle lullabies, or a bedtime story. Some parents like to use a sleep sack or a white noise machine. The key is consistency. When you follow the same sequence every night, your baby will learn to associate these activities with bedtime, making it easier for them to fall asleep. Make sure the environment is conducive to sleep, with a dimly lit room and a comfortable sleep space. The routine helps both you and your baby get into the sleep mindset. Also, make sure the temperature of the room is comfortable for the baby, as your little one will not retain heat in the same manner as adults.

Dealing With Sleep Challenges

Sleep challenges can be frustrating, but they're a common part of parenting. Some babies may experience sleep regressions or difficulties, often around major developmental milestones. The key is to remain patient and adaptable. Stick to your bedtime routine, even if sleep disruptions occur. Be responsive to your baby's needs, whether it's hunger, a diaper change, or comfort. And remember, it's okay to ask for help or take turns with your partner to get some rest. You're in this together, and with time, sleep challenges usually improve.

The sixth month marks a period of remarkable growth in various aspects, encompassing physical, cognitive, and emotional development. Whenever new skills emerge, they can have an impact on your baby's sleep patterns. At this stage, it's common to observe an increase in distracted feedings, which can affect your baby's daily calorie intake and lead to nighttime awakenings due to hunger. Another factor to consider is separation anxiety, which tends to peak between 8 to 10 months but can begin developing around the sixth month or even earlier for certain infants, potentially causing sleep disturbances (Dumaplin, 2023b). Moreover, sleep challenges at six months may indicate that your baby is ready to transition from three naps to two.

COMMUNICATION AND LANGUAGE DEVELOPMENT

Your baby's communication skills are rapidly evolving, as they experiment with babbling and baby talk. These early attempts at interaction are both adorable and essential for their growth. Responding to their sounds, gestures, and attempts to interact is crucial. Engage in conversations with your baby, making them feel heard and valued. These early interactions are the building blocks of language development, setting the stage for effective communication in the future.

Babbling and Baby Talk

Your baby will start to babble and make delightful, albeit nonsensical, sounds. They might repeat simple syllables like "ba-ba" or "da-da." Encourage this by responding to their babbling with enthusiasm. Join in the conversation by babbling back, imitating their sounds. Give them 8-10 seconds to respond to you. This playful interaction is like a mini-language lesson and strengthens the foundation for real words later on.

Responding to Sounds and Voices

Your baby's hearing is well-developed, and they're starting to recognize familiar voices and sounds. Talk to them frequently, even narrate your daily activities. Point out objects and name them to help your baby associate words with real-world items. Sing songs, read stories, and engage them in conversations, even if they can't reply with words yet. This fosters their listening skills and understanding of language.

Nonverbal Communication

Babies communicate not only through sounds but also through gestures, facial expressions, and body language. Pay attention to these cues. If your baby reaches for something, hand it to them. If they smile, smile back. This reciprocal interaction teaches them about cause and effect, essential for language development. It also strengthens your emotional connection.

Encouraging Language Development

Keep communication a central part of your daily routine. Describe the world around your baby, express emotions, and use simple words and phrases. As your baby grows, you can introduce more complex words. Reading to them regularly is incredibly beneficial. Choose books with colorful pictures and simple texts. Even if they don't fully grasp the story, they'll be captivated by the sounds of your voice and the rhythm of the words. This not only fosters language development but also creates a strong bond between you and your little one. When you read stories aloud to your baby, they are exposed to more words, which helps them develop their language skills. By hearing a variety of words, their vocabulary expands, giving them a stronger foundation for speaking. Research shows that children who are regularly spoken to and read to by their parents have a larger vocabulary by the age of 2 compared to those who do not receive this kind of interaction (*Reading Books to Babies*, n.d.).

BABYPROOFING ESSENTIALS

With your baby's newfound mobility comes the need for thorough babyproofing. Your little explorer is eager to crawl, and their curiosity knows no bounds. Creating a safe space for them to move around and learn is paramount. Implement safety measures at home and outdoors to protect your baby as they embark on new adventures. Babyproofing ensures a secure environment where your child can safely explore the world around them, and you can have peace of mind as they do so.

Exploring and Crawling: Creating a Safe Space

When your little one begins to crawl and explore, it's crucial to establish a safe environment. Remember when we talked about "dad-proofing" in Chapter 3? Start by addressing the big safety concerns in your home, such as fixing broken windows, ensuring working smoke detectors, and checking for potential lead paint in older homes (Bykofsky, 2023). This foundational safety maintenance sets the stage for a secure living space.

Additionally, focus on furniture safety, particularly in the nursery and living areas. Secure heavy or unstable furniture to prevent tipping and look for child-friendly options like rounded coffee tables and soft ottomans with storage. These measures protect your child from potential falls and collisions, ensuring a safe space for their crawling and exploration.

Safety Measures at Home and Outdoors

Consider safety measures both inside and outside your home. Childproof the kitchen with cabinet locks to prevent access to harmful items, and use cordless blinds to eliminate strangulation hazards. Supervise bath times closely, as drowning can occur even in shallow water.

In the bathroom and laundry room, store medications and cleaning supplies out of reach. Look for potential choking hazards from your child's perspective and address them proactively. Regularly assess your home for safety, keeping it age-appropriate as your child grows and develops. Consulting experts or resources like poison control can provide guidance when needed, ensuring your home remains a secure space for your little one.

DAD'S WORKOUT

- Babyproofing can be a workout in itself. Turn it into a dance routine. Dodge the hazardous areas while dancing to your baby's favorite tunes.
- Turn everyday activities like diaper changes and mealtime into impromptu dance sessions, introducing your baby to the joy of music and rhythm.
- Babbling Burpee Blitz: A high-energy, multitasking workout! Respond to your baby's adorable babbling with burpees—each "ba-ba" or "da-da" they say means a burpee for you! Baby's your new personal trainer!

CHAPTER 9
CREATING LASTING MEMORIES WITH YOUR GROWING BABY

" *I think [parenthood] brings out the child in all of us. That's what's so beautiful. It reminds you of the fascination you had with things, and how you can spend hours just being with someone. It's amazing.*

CHRIS HEMSWORTH

A s your baby continues to grow and thrive, it's essential to celebrate each moment along the way. Chapter 9 delves into the art of commemorating your child's achievements and fostering a deep bond with them. It's about recognizing that even the smallest steps in their development deserve your attention and applause. By mindfully observing their progress and celebrating the little victories, you not only build a strong connection but also create memories that will last a lifetime. This chapter will guide you on how to engage in playtime as a memorable bonding experience. You'll also learn how to document your baby's growth journey creatively, using photos, videos, and journals to preserve these precious moments.

EMBRACING EVERY ACHIEVEMENT, NO MATTER HOW SMALL

Mindful Observations

Mindfulness is a mental practice and state of awareness that involves focusing your attention on the present moment, without judgment or distraction. It's about being fully present in the here and now, acknowledging your thoughts, feelings, sensations, and the environment around you with an open and accepting attitude. Taking your time is of the utmost importance when it comes to engaging with babies. They have no concept of rushing, and the passage of time means very little to them (*Mindfulness Practice With Babies*, 2021). Babies are wholly absorbed in the present moment. The closer we can get to their innate sense of being in the now, the more effectively we can establish connections with our little ones, nurture trust and mutual understanding, and genuinely relish each and every precious moment and experience.

Let us share with you the wonderful practice of baby gazing. It's that affectionate and proud look dads often give their children, especially when they're playing or achieving milestones. Baby gazing is all about deep observation, which is at the core of being with a baby. It's a profound connection that can change and grow within us as we silently observe our little ones. When we observe without judgment, without comparing, and without evaluating, something special happens. We connect with our babies and feel their essence in that very moment. It's all about being present with our babies, noticing their tiny movements, gestures, and unique ways of being. We accept them just as they are, with no need to fix or change anything. In essence, we're tuning into our baby's heart.

Finding Joy in Every Step

We've got some advice to share about embracing every achievement, no matter how small, in your baby's journey. Finding joy in every step of your child's journey is not only beneficial for their well-being but also incredibly rewarding for you as a parent. Here's what we've learned:

- **Create a Nurturing Atmosphere**: One of the best things you can do for your baby is to create a loving and supportive environment. Celebrate those little achievements; it makes your baby feel encouraged and appreciated. This positive energy is like sunshine for their growth and development.
- **Reduced Stress:** Focusing on the small wins and celebrating them can alleviate stress. It shifts your attention from constantly worrying about your child's progress to appreciating the present moment, which can be a great stress reliever.
- **Respect Their Unique Path**: Every baby is different, so avoid comparing your child's progress to others. Embrace the small milestones that are unique to your

little one. Recognize and value their individual journey, and don't rush them through it.

- **Encourage a Love for Learning**: When you cheer for your baby's tiny victories, you're teaching them to enjoy the process of learning. They'll grow up with curiosity and the belief that effort and determination are worth the celebration, no matter the outcome.

- **Boost Their Confidence**: Celebrating the little things can give your baby a boost of self-esteem. They'll learn that what they do matters, and that's a big confidence builder. This newfound self-assurance will help them face life's challenges with a strong, positive attitude.

- **Positive Outlook on Life**: Embracing every achievement helps your baby develop a positive outlook on life. It's all about appreciating the journey rather than fixating on the destination. This mindset will serve them well as they navigate life's ups and downs.

- **Increased Patience:** Recognizing and celebrating your baby's little victories can teach you patience. It reminds you that development takes time, and it's a gradual process. This patience can spill over into other aspects of your life, making you a more understanding and composed parent.

- **Cherish Everyday Moments**: Don't wait for the big milestones to celebrate; everyday accomplishments like their first step, a new word, or feeding themselves are all cause for joy.

- **Build a Supportive Circle**: Share the joy of your baby's achievements with friends and family. It creates a supportive community around your child, reinforcing their sense of accomplishment. It also encourages others to join in celebrating the small victories. Celebrating your baby's milestones can also bring your family and friends closer to you, creating a supportive network. Their involvement and enthusiasm can provide valuable assistance and encouragement when you need it most.

Building Connection

Celebrating the small milestones of your baby is more than just a way to acknowledge those moments in your child's life; it's about creating a stronger bond within your family. This shared happiness, the memories you create, and the trust you establish with your child can form the foundation of a warm and loving family dynamic. Moreover, celebrating these milestones together with your partner enhances your relationship, nurtures teamwork, and demonstrates your dedication to each other and the journey of parenthood.

MAKING PLAYTIME A MEMORABLE BONDING EXPERIENCE

Playtime with your little one is an incredible opportunity to create lasting memories and strengthen your bond.

Shared Laughter and Joy

Playtime is all about laughter and joy. Engage in those silly sounds, games, and interactions that can make your baby giggle and chuckle. Shared laughter is like glue for your emotional connection. When your baby sees you having fun and being goofy, it creates a sense of warmth and trust.

Get the Baby Outside

Don't forget the importance of getting your baby out into the world. Taking them for walks, to the park, or even out to dinner around others is not just a change of scenery—it's an essential part of their social development. Getting them accustomed to different environments and people early on will pay off in the long run. It helps them become comfortable and adaptable little explorers. Plus, it can be a great way for you to connect as a family and introduce your baby to new experiences together.

DOCUMENTING GROWTH THROUGH PHOTOS AND MEMORIES

Documenting your baby's growth journey is a wonderful way to treasure the moments and reflect on the incredible journey you and your little one are embarking upon.

Creating Lasting Memories

You're on an amazing journey with your baby, and it's important to find creative ways to document this precious time. These memories will become a treasured legacy for both you and your child. Each approach offers a unique way to document the journey and provides you with a reminder of how far you've come.

- **Scrapbook:** A physical scrapbook can be a hands-on way to compile memories. You can add photos, notes, and mementos, creating a tangible keepsake that you and your baby can look back on together. We are big fans of the timeless tradition of the old-school scrapbook.
- **Hand Print or Foot Print Mold:** There's something incredibly special about holding your baby's tiny hand or foot in your own hand. The feeling of those small, wrinkly feet and the strong grip of their little fingers is a memory that will stay with you forever. By creating

hand and footprint molds, you can freeze that moment in time (McMaster, 2019). These molds are not just keepsakes; they are tangible reminders of the beauty of your baby's first moments.

- **Digital Photo Album:** Digital albums are convenient and easily shareable with friends and family. You can organize your photos and videos by age or milestones, making it easy to reminisce about your baby's growth.
- **Dedicated Social Media Account:** Creating a private or family-only social media account allows you to share your baby's journey with loved ones while maintaining a level of privacy (Kim, 2021). It's a modern way to keep everyone updated and connected.
- **First-Year Baby Clothes Quilt:** We all have a favorite onesie or baby blanket that holds a special place in our hearts. But keeping these items stored away may not be the most creative way to preserve your memories. Instead, consider transforming these beloved clothing items into patches for a quilt. This quilt not only reminds you of your baby's early days but also serves a practical purpose. You can snuggle up in it or pass it down as a cherished heirloom to keep the memory of your baby's first year alive.

Capturing Precious Moments

You'll be amazed at how quickly your baby changes, so take the time to document not just the major milestones but also the everyday, incredibly endearing, and seemingly insignificant moments.

- **Videos:** Record videos to capture your baby's first steps, babbling, or moments of discovery. Videos allow you to revisit not just the visuals but also the sounds, expressions, and emotions of those moments.
- **Photos:** Take countless photos of your baby. There's no such thing as too many. They grow so fast, and each snapshot is a snapshot of time, showing their progress. Make sure to include both candid shots and planned photoshoots to capture a wide range of expressions and milestones.
- **Journals:** Writing down your thoughts and experiences as a parent can be a beautiful way to preserve your memories. Journals can provide a detailed account of your baby's growth journey and your own emotions and insights along the way.

Reflecting on the Journey

Schedule dedicated moments to go through the memories you've documented. This reflection allows you to appreciate the growth, the challenges you've overcome, and the unbreakable bond you've formed with your child.

- **Regular Check-Ins:** Parenting challenges you, pushes your boundaries and helps you discover new strengths. Recognize how it has shaped you into a more patient, empathetic, and resilient person. Revisit your documented memories regularly, perhaps on special occasions like birthdays or anniversaries.

- **Share the Memories:** Share these memories with your child as they grow older. Watching videos, looking through photos, and reading journal entries together can be a heartwarming way to connect and reflect on the journey you've shared.
- **Express Gratitude:** Take time to express gratitude for the experience of parenthood. Reflect on the joy, love, and personal growth it has brought into your life. Recognize your role as a nurturing, loving, and dedicated parent. Count your blessings and acknowledge the joy your baby brings into your life.

DAD'S WORKOUT

- Understand the dad equation: Love + Effort + Mindfulness = Epic Dad Win!
- Gather your loved ones and have a baby milestone celebration party—it's like team-building for the whole family!
- Transform everyday routines into unforgettable moments by cheering on your little one's tiny triumphs, from their first wobbly step to those adorable new words.

CHAPTER 10
EXPLORING INDEPENDENCE: BABY'S DEVELOPMENT AT 8-12 MONTHS

> *Fatherhood is the greatest thing that could ever happen. You can't explain it until it happens—it's like telling someone what water feels like before they've ever swam in it.*

MICHAEL BUBLÉ

W elcome to Chapter 10, where we explore the dynamic phase of your baby's development from 8 to 12 months. This period is a tornado of milestones, as your little one starts taking their first steps toward independence. As a father, you play a big role in guiding them through this exciting journey. From those adorable first steps to developing fine motor skills, cognitive leaps, and emotional expressions, we'll delve into it all. We'll also cover the exciting world of transitioning to table foods, understanding their evolving sleep patterns, and nurturing their language skills. Additionally, we'll share insights on fostering social bonds and dealing with separation anxiety as your baby becomes more aware of their surroundings.

CRAWLING TO WALKING: MOTOR MILESTONES

During these months, your baby is on the brink of a world-altering transformation. They are making their way from being a little crawler to a wobbly walker. It's a time filled with incredible milestones that you should celebrate.

- **Crawling and Beyond:** The transition from being a stationary baby to an active crawler is a remarkable feat. Celebrate these first ventures into mobility. Your baby is now able to explore their surroundings, and it's an exciting time to watch them discover the world around them. Give them the freedom to crawl and investigate, but always make sure their environment is safe.
- **Standing Up:** As your baby gains strength and balance, they'll start pulling themselves up to a standing position. This newfound ability opens up a whole new world for them. Encourage their efforts and make sure to baby-proof your home, so they can practice standing without worry.

- **Those First Steps:** When those first steps come, it's a momentous occasion. Your baby's first independent steps are a culmination of months of effort and determination. Be there to support and celebrate this achievement. Hold out your arms and let them take those wobbly steps toward you, offering words of encouragement and claps of joy.

DEVELOPING FINE MOTOR SKILLS: PINCER GRASP AND HAND-EYE COORDINATION

Developing fine motor skills, particularly the pincer grasp and hand-eye coordination, is a vital aspect of your baby's growth and early childhood development.

Pincer Grasp

The pincer grasp is a fine motor skill that involves using the thumb and forefinger to pick up small objects or manipulate items with precision. It's a valuable skill, as it enables your baby to perform various tasks, from self-feeding to playing with small toys. Here's how you can encourage and support the development of the pincer grasp:

- **Offer Appropriate Toys:** Provide toys and objects that are specifically designed to encourage the use of the pincer grasp. Toys with small parts, building blocks, or stacking rings are excellent choices. These items require your baby to use their thumb and forefinger to pick up and manipulate them.

- **Practice With Food:** During mealtime, encourage your baby to self-feed with finger foods like peas, Cheerios, or small pieces of fruit. This not only helps develop their pincer grasp but also fosters independence as they learn to feed themselves.
- **Play Peek-a-Boo:** Play games like peek-a-boo with small toys or objects hidden under a cloth. Encourage your baby to uncover the items using their pincer grasp. This activity promotes hand-eye coordination and fine motor skills.

Hand-Eye Coordination

Hand-eye coordination is the ability to coordinate visual information with hand movements. It's a fundamental skill that enables your baby to perform tasks that involve precise hand movements and visual tracking. Here's how you can help your baby develop hand-eye coordination:

- **Engage in Interactive Play:** Play interactive games that involve hand-eye coordination, such as building with blocks, stacking toys, or playing with shape sorters. These activities require your baby to align their hand movements with what they see.

- **Read Together:** Reading books with colorful illustrations and pointing out objects on the page helps your baby practice visual tracking. Encourage them to touch the pictures as you name them, fostering a connection between what they see and their hand movements.
- **Play With Balls:** Rolling and catching soft balls or lightweight objects is a great way to improve hand-eye coordination. Start with simple rolling games and progress to gentle tossing and catching as your baby grows.

- **Art and Drawing:** Provide your baby with large crayons or markers and let them explore scribbling on paper. This activity helps refine their hand-eye coordination as they learn to control their hand movements to create lines and shapes.
- **Mirror Play:** Use a mirror during playtime to help your baby develop hand-eye coordination. Encourage them to reach for their reflection and touch it. This activity not only engages their visual tracking but also introduces them to the concept of cause and effect.

COGNITIVE LEAPS: PROBLEM-SOLVING AND CAUSE-AND-EFFECT

As a parent, it's essential to recognize the importance of your baby's cognitive leaps, especially when it comes to their problem-solving abilities and understanding cause-and-effect relationships. These skills serve as the building blocks for their future learning and critical thinking, so let's foster their growth in a way that's both safe and enjoyable.

Start by creating a secure environment for your little explorer, where they can freely touch and investigate their surroundings. Ensure that your home is baby-proofed to keep potential hazards at bay during their curious phase.

Engage in interactive play that ignites their curiosity and tickles their senses. Games like peek-a-boo, stacking blocks, or simple puzzles can introduce problem-solving and cause-and-effect concepts in a way that's both fun and educational.

Don't forget to include sensory play in their daily routine, offering textured toys, colorful objects, and items of different shapes and sizes. Allowing your baby to explore, touch, grab, and examine objects is how they begin to understand the world around them.

As your baby grows, introduce age-appropriate challenges that encourage problem-solving. Be their patient and encouraging guide as they develop these cognitive skills.

Reading together is a wonderful way to introduce your baby to the world of problem-solving and cause-and-effect while showing them how you tackle challenges through your actions is a powerful way for them to learn by watching.

All of these early experiences will set the stage for their future cognitive development, nurturing their curiosity and paving the way for their critical thinking abilities.

EXPRESSING EMOTIONS: UNDERSTANDING BABY'S SIGNALS

Understanding and responding to your baby's signals and emotions is a vital aspect of parenting. This connection is at the core of building a strong and loving relationship with your little one. Understanding and responding to your baby's emotions is a beautiful journey that deepens your bond and helps your child feel loved and secure. It's a two-way street where you'll learn to interpret their signals, and they'll learn to trust your presence and care. Here's some guidance on expressing and interpreting your baby's emotions:

- **Nonverbal Communication:** Even as your baby grows, nonverbal communication remains a significant part of their expression. They may use gestures, facial expressions, and vocalizations to convey their emotions and needs. Pay close attention to these cues to understand what they're trying to tell you.
- **Vocalization:** By this age, your baby may have developed a broader range of vocal sounds. They may babble, giggle, or even say their first words. Listen to their vocalizations to gauge their mood and interests. Encourage their attempts at communication by responding and engaging in conversation.
- **Crying:** While crying may still be a way of expressing discomfort, hunger, or tiredness, it can also signify frustration or a desire for attention. Pay attention to the nuances in their cries and try to identify the cause. Respond promptly to provide comfort and reassurance. We found that high-pitched crying was from some form of pain/discomfort being felt, while a lower range of crying was more in line with "feed me."
- **Gestures and Pointing:** Many babies in this age range begin to use gestures and pointing to indicate what they want or what interests them. They might point to a toy they want to play with or reach out for something they find intriguing. Encourage this form of communication by acknowledging and responding to their gestures.

- **Social Engagement:** Your baby is becoming more social and may exhibit signs of attachment and separation anxiety. They might cling to you or show distress when you leave the room. Reassure them with a comforting tone and let them know you'll be back. Encourage your children to spend time with others and promote social interactions by making sure they are around other kids or people. Ensure you take those date nights and have a family member or babysitter watch them. While they may still cling, it will help build those social skills to eventually help reduce the clinginess.

- **Playful Interactions:** Engage in playful interactions that encourage emotional expression. Peek-a-boo, tickling, and imitating their babbling are excellent ways to create joyful moments and strengthen your emotional connection. Don't be afraid to be weird! Let your inner child out!

- **Responsive Parenting:** Being a responsive parent remains crucial. Respond to their needs, whether it's a diaper change, feeding, or simply wanting to be held. This responsive approach fosters trust and a sense of security.

- **Encourage Independence:** As your baby approaches their first birthday, they may begin exploring their newfound independence. Encourage this by providing safe opportunities for them to practice their newfound skills. Simple tasks like self-feeding or choosing a toy to play with can boost their self-esteem.

- **Talk to Your Baby:** Continue talking to your baby, even if they don't yet understand all your words. Your conversations foster language development and emotional connection. Describe your actions, ask questions, and listen to their responses to promote communication. It doesn't have to be all goos and gahs; talk to them like they are your buddy!

NUTRITIONAL ADVENTURES: TRANSITIONING TO TABLE FOODS

Transitioning your baby to table foods is an exciting and important phase in their development. Graduating from purees and introducing different textures is a significant milestone. Here's how you can make this nutritional adventure a smooth and enriching journey, all while embracing the mess:

Graduating From Purees: Introducing Textures

It's time to move beyond purees! This allows your baby to explore various textures and flavors. Be ready for some mess; it's all part of the learning process. Let them touch, taste, and experience different foods. Around 9-10 months, start offering soft finger foods. Pieces of ripe banana, small cubes of cheese, or well-cooked pasta can encourage self-feeding and fine motor skills. Always watch your baby closely to prevent choking. Encourage your baby to feed themselves and participate in mealtimes. These experiences help build a sense of autonomy and confidence. While it may take some patience, it's an important step toward them becoming more self-reliant.

Self-Feeding

Your baby may start showing an interest in feeding themselves with their fingers or trying to use a spoon. Encourage this newfound independence by offering appropriate utensils and letting them practice, even if it gets a bit messy.

Variety of Textures

As they venture into solid foods, your baby is likely becoming more comfortable with a variety of textures. Progress from purees to more lumpy or mashed foods to encourage chewing and speech development.

Age-Appropriate Foods and Portion Sizes

Be mindful of providing foods that are suitable for your baby's age and developmental stage. Start with simple, soft foods like mashed vegetables, fruits, or well-cooked pasta. Avoid giving honey to babies under one year old, as it can carry the risk of infant botulism. Offer appropriate portion sizes, ensuring they have enough to satisfy their hunger without overfeeding. Portion sizes can vary from baby to baby, but generally, start with small amounts and let your baby's appetite guide you. Babies have tiny tummies, so they won't eat much at each meal. A tablespoon or two of each food is often sufficient.

Navigating Picky Eating

Picky eating is a common phase in a baby's development. They may show preferences for certain foods or reject others. The key is to remain patient and keep offering a variety of nutritious options. Continue to introduce new flavors and textures, and be a role model by enjoying a diverse diet yourself.

Balancing Breastfeeding or Formula With Solid Foods

As your baby transitions to solid foods, you can gradually reduce their reliance on breast milk or formula. Work toward introducing alternative cups for drinking. It may take attempts with a few different types of cups for them to "get it." Also, this process can take some time and can become frustrating; stick to it! They will eventually find a type of cup that works for them and transition away from the bottle.

The transition from breastfeeding or formula to exclusively solid foods is a gradual process that varies from one baby to another. There is no fixed timeline, as it depends on the baby's individual development and readiness. Some babies may still receive breast milk or formula as their primary source of nutrition until around 12 months or longer. Others may transition to solids more quickly and gradually reduce their milk intake.

SLEEP PATTERNS AND NAP TRANSITION

Sleep Changes in the Second Half of the First Year

As your baby progresses through their first year, you'll notice significant changes in their sleep patterns. They may begin to sleep for longer stretches at night and take fewer, longer naps during the day.

Transitioning From Multiple Naps to Fewer Naps

Navigating your baby's sleep patterns and the transition from multiple naps to fewer naps can be a rewarding yet challenging journey. Typically, babies transition from multiple short naps to fewer, longer naps as they grow. This transition varies from baby to baby. Pay attention to your baby's cues to determine when they are ready for fewer naps. A common shift is from three naps to two naps a day.

Nurturing Healthy Sleep Habits

- **Establish Consistent Routines:** Routines provide a sense of security for your baby. Maintain a consistent sleep schedule, mealtime routine, and playtime rituals. Predictable patterns help your baby feel confident and comforted, and they signal when it's time to sleep.
- **Create a Soothing Bedtime Routine:** A calming bedtime routine can signal to your baby that it's time to wind down. Activities like a warm bath, reading a book, or gentle rocking can help prepare them for sleep.
- **Provide a Comfortable Sleep Environment:** Ensure that your baby's sleep environment is safe and comfortable. The room should be dark, quiet, and at a comfortable temperature. Use a sleep sack or wearable blanket to keep your baby warm without loose bedding.

Sleep Challenges and Solutions

We discussed some sleep challenges around the six-month mark in Chapter 8. Sleep challenges at 6 months and 12 months can differ significantly due to the developmental changes and growth that occur during this period.

- **Fewer Night Wakings:** By 12 months, many babies have developed the ability to sleep for longer stretches at night. While some may still wake occasionally, it's generally less frequent than at 6 months. Night feedings may become less necessary as solid food intake increases.

- **Nap Transition:** Babies at 12 months often transition from three or four naps to two naps a day. This shift can lead to longer awake periods between naps and better-defined nap times. Try to shoot for nap windows and don't skip naps! You may have to adjust your schedule around naps; we tried to target a morning and mid-afternoon nap. If we missed one, the crankiness set in and the rest of the day was a bust.
- **Increasing Independence:** As babies approach their first birthday, they may start to show signs of sleep independence. They might be more inclined to self-soothe and fall asleep without as much parental assistance.
- **Teething Challenges:** Teething can continue to be a factor in sleep disturbances, but by 12 months, most babies have more teeth, and they might be better at handling teething discomfort.
- **Behavioral Sleep Challenges:** As babies become toddlers, they can develop sleep behavior patterns, such as bedtime resistance or bedtime stalling. They might assert their independence by testing limits at bedtime.
- **Nightmares and Night Terrors:** Some children may start experiencing nightmares or night terrors around 12 months. These episodes can disrupt sleep and require parental comfort and reassurance.

COMMUNICATION AND LANGUAGE EXPLORATION

First Words: Babbling to Meaningful Speech

You're also setting the example here. This is the time to clean up the language, ensure communication at home is positive and nurturing, and support them in building a vocabulary. Babies take in their surroundings much more than we know, so set the example!

Understanding Gestures and Nonverbal Communication

Pay attention to your baby's gestures and non-verbal cues. These can be subtle but are essential forms of communication. When they point, reach, or use eye contact, respond to their cues. This fosters their sense of being understood and valued.

Encouraging Language Development Through Interaction

Your baby's interactions are becoming more interactive. Engage in two-way play, such as rolling a ball back and forth or imitating their actions. This reciprocal engagement builds a strong parent-child bond and reinforces the concept of turn-taking, which is a fundamental aspect of communication.

Imitative Play

Babies love to imitate actions they see, like pretending to talk on a toy phone or feeding a stuffed animal (Taylor, 2021). Encourage this imitative play. It's not just fun; it's a way for them to explore and mimic the world around them, and it can also be a playful introduction to language and communication.

Pretend play can:

- **Foster Self-Control Skills:** Engaging in imaginative play promotes the development of self-control skills. When children play make-believe, they must collaborate to agree on pretend scenarios and decide on their roles. This can sometimes lead to frustrating emotions, and it's an opportunity for toddlers and preschoolers to learn how to manage these feelings.
- **Cultivate Relationships:** Creating imaginary worlds through play brings children closer to one another and deepens their understanding of their playmates. When parents participate in pretend play, it encourages interactive exchanges that strengthen the bonds between children and caregivers.
- **Explore Complex Emotions:** Pretend play provides a safe space for children to explore and navigate difficult or scary situations, such as visiting the doctor or starting daycare or preschool. Through imaginative scenarios, they can work through their emotions and fears.

- **Enhance Language and Communication Skills:**
  Dreaming up scenarios and negotiating the rules of play requires the use of more advanced language and ideas. This process promotes the development of language and communication skills as children articulate their thoughts and ideas during play.

Exploration of Objects

Your baby is entering the phase of more complex exploration, such as fitting objects into containers and dumping them out. Use this as an opportunity for language development. Describe the actions and objects they're interacting with. For example, "You're putting the block into the bucket, and now you're taking it out!"

READING AND SINGING: BUILDING A LOVE FOR WORDS

Let's talk about the incredible world of baby babbling, books, and belting out songs. You see, at this age, your little one is like a tiny language sponge, soaking up everything. Reading and singing offer several advantages to babies in this age group. Firstly, they aid in language development by exposing babies to a wide range of words, sounds, and tones, facilitating the expansion of their language skills.

Additionally, engaging in reading and singing stimulates cognitive development (Tanguay, 2018). The wacky and colorful pictures in those baby books are like a visual playground for their little noggin. Plus, those catchy rhymes in songs? They're brain candy, making your baby focus and groove. Furthermore, these activities provide a wonderful opportunity for bonding. Sharing books and songs creates a special one-on-one time that strengthens the emotional connection between you and your baby.

Moreover, reading and singing offer sensory stimulation through different textures and materials in books that babies can touch and explore. This tactile engagement is beneficial for their sensory development, and singing exposes them to various sounds and rhythms, enhancing their auditory senses. Establishing a routine of reading and singing can also provide a sense of comfort and predictability for your baby. They learn that these activities are enjoyable and occur regularly, offering reassurance and comfort. So go ahead, serenade your baby with "Twinkle, Twinkle Little Star" or explore colorful textures in those touchy-feely books.

Ultimately, reading and singing help foster a love for words and books in your baby. They begin to associate books and songs with pleasure and positive emotions, laying the foundation for a lifelong passion for learning and reading. So, keep the rhymes rolling and the books coming. To maximize the benefits, choose age-appropriate books with colorful images and simple text, engage in interactive reading, and make singing a joyful shared experience for both you and your baby.

NURTURING SOCIAL SKILLS AND RELATIONSHIPS

Building Social Bonds: Interaction with Family and Peers

Your baby is a little people person in the making. Encourage social connections with family members and peers. Let them spend time with grandparents, aunts, uncles, and other babies. These interactions lay the foundation for healthy social skills.

Sharing and Turn-Taking: Encouraging Cooperation

Babies love sharing, but they also love keeping toys to themselves. Teach the art of sharing and turn-taking early on. It can be as simple as taking turns rolling a ball or sharing a favorite stuffed animal. When your baby cooperates, offer positive reinforcement. Use enthusiastic praise and smiles to let them know they're doing a great job. Positive reinforcement encourages them to repeat the behavior (Souders, 2019).

Separation Anxiety: Navigating Baby's Emotional Development

Be ready for a bout of separation anxiety. When your little one starts getting clingy, it's just their way of saying, "I love you so much!" So, reassure them, but also gently introduce the idea that it's okay for you to step away for a bit. They'll learn that you always come back, and it's a vital part of their emotional growth.

Attachment

The parent-baby bond is like a superglue connection. Your baby relies on you for comfort and care. Be there for them, respond to their needs, and hold them close. This attachment forms the basis of trust and security for a lifetime.

There are different attachment styles, and they're usually formed in childhood based on how our caregivers responded to our needs. These styles can stick with us into adulthood and affect how we interact in relationships. For parents, understanding attachment style is important, as it can influence your relationship with your child and their future relationships.

There are different types of attachment styles:

- **Secure Attachment:** If your child has a secure attachment, they feel comfortable knowing you're there for them. They trust that you'll respond when they need you, and they can express their feelings without fear of rejection (Robinson, 2019).
- **Anxious Attachment:** Kids with an anxious attachment style may worry more about being left alone or not being loved enough. They might need lots of reassurance and worry when things change in your relationship.
- **Avoidant Attachment:** Children with an avoidant attachment might be more independent and find it challenging to open up emotionally. They might keep their distance because they're afraid of getting hurt.

- **Disorganized Attachment:** This one is a bit complicated. Kids with a disorganized attachment style may have experienced inconsistent or confusing caregiving. This can make their relationships more challenging and unpredictable.

Fostering Positive Social Interactions

You're not just raising a baby; you're raising a future friend, sibling, and family member. Your baby is a social sponge, absorbing how to interact from you. Model positive social behavior, like using please and thank you or greeting others warmly. They learn from your actions, so set a good example.

DAD'S WORKOUT

- Boost your kid's IQ and happiness quotient by being a dad who's all in.
- Shape the future: One epic blanket fort at a time, fostering the next generation of architects.
- Baby juggling: Master the art of multitasking by juggling baby bottles, diapers, and toys while trying to maintain your sanity—it's a workout that'll make you feel like you're in the parenting Olympics!

CHAPTER 11
BALANCING WORK, FAMILY, AND SELF-CARE

" *Success, and even life itself, wouldn't be worth anything if I didn't have my children by my side. They mean everything to me.*

JUDE LAW

In Chapter 11, we address a topic that resonates with many fathers—balancing work, family, and self-care. It's vital to find harmony among your responsibilities while nurturing your well-being. The work-family dynamic can be a delicate dance, and in this chapter, we'll explore strategies for managing this balance effectively.

Additionally, we'll delve into the world of self-care and how carving out moments for yourself can recharge your spirit. Furthermore, we'll explore the changing landscape of your social dynamics as you embrace your role as a father. Join us as we navigate the intricate tapestry of work, family, and self-care. Your role as a loving father is at the center of this intricate dance.

MANAGING RESPONSIBILITIES AND WELL-BEING

Balancing your work and family roles is essential for your overall well-being. It ensures that you can be present and engaged with your family while fulfilling your work responsibilities.

Navigating the Work-Family Dynamic

The work-family dynamic is all about finding the right balance between your job and your family. It means juggling the responsibilities of your career while making sure you're present for those special family moments. It's a constant process of fine-tuning, so stay flexible, communicate openly with your employer and family, and be ready to adapt as your family grows and your career evolves. Balancing both sides of the equation is key to a happy and fulfilling life.

Prioritizing Family

Maintaining a healthy work-life balance should be a top priority. It's crucial to understand that your family's well-being and quality time with your loved ones are just as important as your professional commitments (Wolf, 2021). Make a conscious effort to plan quality time with your family. This could include activities such as family outings or simply having dinner together. Prioritize these moments and make them a priority in your schedule.

Open Communication

Effective communication with your employer about your family commitments and needs is key. It helps create understanding and flexibility in managing your work responsibilities. Inquire with your employer or manager upon returning to work about the guidelines regarding taking care of ill children (Novak, 2020). Is it possible for you to work remotely (if you're not already doing so)? Can you have a flexible work schedule? Similarly, it is important to discuss your baby's doctor appointments. If you require two hours for a regular appointment, can you compensate for the time in the future?

Also, regularly communicate with your family about your work commitments and involve them in decision-making processes. This will help them understand your responsibilities and foster a supportive environment.

Flexibility and Boundaries

Here's a practical tip from someone who's been through it: Think of your work and family life like two separate time slots on your calendar. Set clear boundaries to protect your family time. It's like drawing a line between work and play, ensuring you're fully present with your little one. It's a simple but effective way to balance your responsibilities. Enjoy those precious moments with your family!

Be Present

Amid the hustle and bustle of work and other commitments, practice mindfulness and be fully present with your baby. Engaging in one-on-one interactions, playtime, and cuddles is a precious gift that nurtures their emotional well-being. When you're truly in the moment, you create a strong connection with your child, building beautiful memories that will last a lifetime. Embrace the present, savor these special moments, and watch your bond with your baby grow even stronger.

FINDING MOMENTS OF SELF-CARE AND RECHARGING

Self-Care Importance

Recognize the importance of self-care for your own well-being. Taking care of yourself enables you to be a better parent and partner.

Carving Out Time

If we've learned anything, it's that free time doesn't present itself. You have to find it. Discover ways to find small pockets of time for self-care within your busy schedule. Even brief moments of self-indulgence can make a big difference.

Carving out time for yourself as a new dad can be challenging, but it's super important for your well-being and your ability to be present for your family. Here are some practical tips to help you make it happen:

- **Set Priorities:** Recognize that self-care is not selfish; it's necessary for your overall health and happiness. Make it a priority.
- **Plan and Schedule:** Just like you schedule work meetings or family activities, schedule time for yourself. Block out specific periods on your calendar for self-care.
- **Share Responsibilities:** Discuss with your partner how you can share responsibilities effectively. This may

include taking turns watching the baby to allow each other some personal time.

- **Naptime or Bedtime:** Use your baby's naptime or bedtime for personal activities. Whether it's reading a book, watching a show, or pursuing a hobby, these moments can be your sanctuary.

- **Enlist Support:** Reach out to family or friends who can help babysit for a few hours, giving you some free time.

- **Combine Activities:** If possible, combine personal activities with family time. For example, go for a family walk or run, or involve your baby in a hobby you enjoy.

- **Set Boundaries:** Be clear with your family about the importance of your personal time. Let them know when you need a break and ask for their support in respecting your boundaries.

- **Maximize Efficiency:** Make the most of any free moments during the day. If you have a short break while the baby is occupied or sleeping, use that time for your own interests.

- **Self-Care Rituals:** Establish self-care rituals that can be integrated into your daily routine, such as morning meditation, exercise, or journaling.

- **Delegate and Outsource:** Don't hesitate to delegate or outsource tasks that can free up your time, such as hiring a cleaning service or using grocery delivery services.

Recharging Strategies

Recharging strategies are essential for maintaining your well-being as a dad, and one effective method is to embrace some well-deserved "me-time." This designated period offers you the chance to unwind, kick back, and indulge in activities you're passionate about. Explore things that rejuvenate you and provide a mental break from the demands of parenting and work. Whether it's pursuing a hobby you love, going for a long run, or simply enjoying a quiet moment with a book, this time allows you to recharge your batteries and come back to your family feeling refreshed and rejuvenated. This recharging time is essential to keep your energy and spirits up. It's a vital component in the playbook of parenthood that ensures you're at your best for both yourself and your loved ones.

NAVIGATING SOCIAL DYNAMICS AND FRIENDSHIPS

Changing Social Landscape

Brace yourself for the fact that your social life will go through some funny, unpredictable twists and turns. Your party animal days may be a bit quieter now, and your late-night adventures might involve soothing a crying baby rather than barhopping. Your priorities and the time you can spend socializing may shift, but don't feel like you can't get out and do something! Coordinate with your partner, get with some buddies, and have some fun. You may be in by 8 p.m. and asleep by 9 p.m., but, hey, you made time to recharge and that's important!

Prioritizing Connections

As you navigate this new terrain of parenthood, make it a point to surround yourself with pals who get your parenting journey. These friends are like gold—they understand your late-night feedings, diaper dilemmas, and endless baby photo sharing. They'll be your support system and cheerleaders. You'll bond over stories of baby's first steps, diaper disasters, and that magic moment when you both finally get a full night's sleep. So, focus on nurturing these relationships that not only accept but celebrate your role as a dad. After all, these friends are the real MVPs in the adventure of fatherhood!

Creating New Bonds

To make the parenting journey more enjoyable, seek opportunities to connect with other parents who are on a similar crazy adventure. Joining parenting groups or engaging in activities like playdates can be a game-changer. These situations aren't just about your little one making friends; they're about you connecting with other parents. You'll find yourself sharing tales of sleepless nights, diaper blowouts, and those hilarious baby babble conversations. One fantastic way to connect with other parents and strengthen those bonds is by embracing the role of a "Playdate Papa." These are the dads who take the initiative to organize playdates for their kids and their friends. By doing so, you not only provide a fun and interactive environment for your child but also open doors to building lasting friendships with other parents who share the adventure of parenthood. These playdates become the backdrop for shared experiences, laughter, and mutual support, creating a tight-knit network of like-minded dads.

ESTABLISHING A NETWORK OF DAD PEERS

Importance of Community

Recognize the value of connecting with other dads who share your experiences. It's not just about finding companions for your journey; it's about building a support system and a deep sense of belonging. These are the folks who understand that there are days when changing a diaper feels like a wrestling match and moments when your baby's giggles are the greatest symphony in the world.

Seeking Advice and Sharing Experiences

Exchange insights, challenges, and tips with fellow fathers. Learning from others can make your fatherhood journey more manageable and enjoyable. Parenting can be overwhelming, especially for first-time dads. Sharing experiences with fellow fathers reassures you that you are not alone in your struggles. Hearing that others have faced similar difficulties and triumphed can reduce anxiety and provide a sense of normalcy.

Mutual Support

In your community of dads, provide and receive encouragement. Being part of a group that shares common experiences fosters a sense of camaraderie and support. Seeking advice from experienced fathers allows you to tap into a wealth of knowledge and learn from those who have been through similar situations. Whether it's about soothing a fussy baby, managing sleepless nights, or handling diaper blowouts, getting advice can provide practical solutions and boost a new dad's confidence.

STRENGTHENING YOUR IDENTITY AS A FATHER

Fatherhood comes in various flavors, and there's a dad for every occasion (*Dad Tribes*, 2020). You've got your "Shameless Dad" who owns every dad cliche with pride, from snoring on the sofa to sporting cringeworthy aprons. He's the king of TikTok BBQs, much to his kids' horror. Then there's the "Side-line Dad" who believes he's raising the next Tom Brady and is determined to turn weekends into sports boot camp, whether his child likes it or not. Next up, we have the "Action Dad" who's always in athletic mode, showing off calves that look like honey-roast ham. His kids practically live on mountains or swim in freezing lakes every weekend. But let's not forget the noble "Stay-At-Home Dad" who's given up career dreams to be a family man. He may have underestimated the challenge, but his heart is in the right place. Lastly, there's the "Over-Prepared Dad" who's basically a walking baby gadget store. His diaper bag weighs a ton with bottle holsters, motion sensors, and all things "smart." Leaving the house takes an hour, and he's Dadman with his utility belt of baby gear. So, my fellow dad, whichever dad style suits you, embrace it and remember that there's no one-size-fits-all in fatherhood—it's all about finding your groove!

Self-Reflection

In all seriousness—take time to reflect on the changes and personal growth you've experienced as a father. It's important not to lose your own identity in the process. You can continue to nurture your interests and passions, even as you embrace the role of a parent. There's always an opportunity for reevaluation and adaptation. Allocating time for your personal interests isn't self-centered but a form of self-care (Benedictus, n.d.). Whether it's hiking in the mountains or enjoying a book at a quiet cafe, pursuing activities that genuinely make you happy is advantageous for your mental and emotional health. What's particularly significant is that it not only benefits you but also positively impacts your family. Occasionally immersing yourself in what brings you joy can serve as a relief valve, making you a more enjoyable presence when you're at home.

DAD'S WORKOUT

- Seek support from friends, family, and fellow dads; after all, even superheroes have sidekicks.
- Balancing work, family, and self-care is like trying to juggle flaming swords while riding a unicycle— challenging but surprisingly entertaining.
- Finding time for self-care as a new dad is like hunting for hidden gems in the vast jungle of responsibilities, but when you do discover those precious moments, they're worth their weight in gold.

CHAPTER 12
GRADUATING FROM DADDY BOOT CAMP

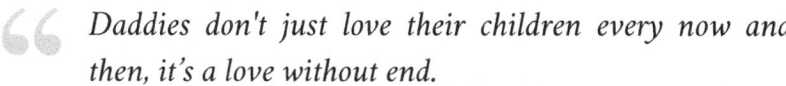 *Daddies don't just love their children every now and then, it's a love without end.*

GEORGE STRAIT

Congratulations, Dad! You've reached a significant milestone as you conclude your first year as a father. Over the past 12 months, you've embarked on a transformative journey, from the anticipation of your baby's arrival to the joyful moments and inevitable challenges that shaped your identity as a loving and devoted dad.

In this final chapter, we invite you to reflect on the incredible progress you've made, both as a father and as an individual. Your baby's growth mirrors your own development, and you'll gain a deeper appreciation for the unique bond you've created along the way.

As your baby takes their first steps into toddlerhood, your role as a father continues to evolve. The confidence and wisdom you've gained from your Daddy Boot Camp experience will serve you well as you navigate the adventures, both big and small, that lie ahead. This chapter also encourages you to celebrate the milestone of your baby's first year, plan a memorable first birthday celebration, and create keepsakes to cherish for years to come. Remember, while your baby's first year has come to a close, the journey of parenthood is an ongoing adventure filled with learning, laughter, and love. You've laid a strong foundation for the years of parenting ahead, and you can move forward with confidence as a proud graduate of Daddy Boot Camp.

THE FIRST FULL YEAR OF YOUR CHILD'S LIFE!

As you celebrate the completion of your baby's first year, it's a time to reminisce about the incredible journey you've embarked upon as a dad. This year has been filled with unforgettable moments, from the first smile to the first steps, and you've been there to witness and cherish each one.

REFLECTING ON YOUR JOURNEY

Acknowledging Growth and Transformation

Looking back on this past year, you can't help but marvel at the transformative journey you've been on, from the anticipation of becoming a father to this moment of reflection. The challenges and joys you've experienced have not only marked your child's growth but also your evolution into a confident and loving father.

A Year of Discovery

This first year has been a profound year of discovery for you. It's been a journey of exploring the depths of your emotions, resilience, and the power of love. You've discovered that your heart can expand to accommodate an immeasurable amount of love for your child, that your patience can endure sleepless nights and endless diaper changes, and that your resilience can withstand the challenges of parenthood. The discoveries have extended beyond the boundaries of your emotions. You've also uncovered a newfound sense of commitment to your child's well-being, both physically and emotionally. You've learned to anticipate their needs, provide comfort, and celebrate their every achievement. In essence, this year has revealed your incredible capacity for love and your unyielding dedication as a father.

Personal and Parental Growth

As you reflect on your baby's development, you'll notice how it mirrors your growth as a father. It's a testament to the profound connection between parent and child. In the moments when your child learned to crawl, you also learned to adapt to a new reality. When they began to express themselves through their first words, you found yourself becoming more patient, understanding, and empathetic. Your child's growth and your personal and parental growth have evolved in tandem, creating a harmonious synergy. This mutual transformation has allowed you to view the world through a fresh set of eyes, both your own and your child's, and has deepened the bond that you share. You've become not just a guide but a lifelong learner, adapting and growing alongside your child as they embark on their own journey of discovery.

Embracing Your Role

Over the past year, your identity as a dad has undergone a beautiful transformation, and it's a transformation worth celebrating. You've embraced your role as a caregiver, protector, teacher, and friend with unwavering dedication. As you've nurtured your child's physical and emotional well-being, you've become their source of comfort and support, their first teacher, and their most trusted confidant. This evolution has formed a unique bond, one that will continue to strengthen as the years go by. Embracing your role as a father is not just about fulfilling responsibilities; it's about cherishing the opportunity to be an integral part of your child's life, guiding them through the world, and witnessing their growth and milestones.

THE ONGOING ADVENTURE

As your baby graduates from the newborn phase and enters toddlerhood, your role as a father continues to evolve. The confidence you've gained from your Daddy Boot Camp experience equips you for the exciting challenges and rewards that lie ahead. Your ongoing adventure as a parent is just beginning, and it's a journey you're well-prepared to face with love and dedication.

Celebrating One Year

Reflecting on the First Year of Parenthood

As you celebrate your baby's first year, it's also an opportunity to reflect on your first year as a parent. The memories, lessons, and love you've experienced are a testament to the strength of your family bond.

Planning a Memorable First Birthday Celebration

Your baby's first birthday is a significant milestone, and it's a chance to create lasting memories. Planning a memorable celebration is a reflection of the love and joy your child has brought into your life.

Here are some ideas to help you create a special and unforgettable birthday party:

- Theme Party: Choose a fun and age-appropriate theme for the party, such as "Barnyard Bash," "Under the Sea," "Safari Adventure," or "Little Prince/Princess." Decorate the venue, cake, and invitations to match the theme.
- Smash Cake: The classic "smash cake" moment is always a hit. Provide a small, separate cake just for your baby to dig into, make a mess, and enjoy. Capture the joy and messiness with lots of photos.
- Balloon Decor: Balloons are a must for any birthday party. Create balloon bouquets, arches, or a balloon wall in coordinating colors or themed shapes.
- Themed Cake and Cupcakes: Order or bake a birthday cake and cupcakes that match the party theme. You can also have cookies, cake pops, or other themed desserts.
- Time Capsule: Have guests write down well wishes or birthday messages for your child, which you can seal in a time capsule to open on a future birthday.
- Live Entertainment: Consider hiring a professional entertainer, like a clown, magician, or puppeteer, to engage the kids and add an element of surprise.

Embracing the Journey Ahead

While your baby's first year has come to a close, remember that the journey of parenthood is an ongoing adventure filled with learning, laughter, and love. As your child grows and explores, you'll continue to guide, support, and cherish every milestone, no matter how big or small. Looking forward to date nights, maintaining a work-life balance, and connecting with your "dad tribe" are all part of the exciting journey ahead. Congratulations, Dad, on successfully navigating your first year of fatherhood, and here's to many more years of love, laughter, and precious memories. Your dedication, love, and commitment have laid a strong foundation for the years of parenting ahead. So go forth with confidence, knowing that you're a graduate of Daddy Boot Camp and a proud father ready for the next chapter of this incredible journey.

DAD'S WORKOUT

- Chase your speedy toddler around the house, and you'll soon be the fastest dad in town! Bonus points for avoiding the Lego minefield.
- Late-Night Stand-Up: Baby's midnight feedings are your prime-time comedy slot. Who cares if the audience is too young to appreciate your jokes? You're building a fan base one baby giggle at a time.
- Laundry Limbo Pro: Finding tiny socks, onesies, and toys in unexpected places is your specialty. It's a never-ending laundry limbo, and you're the reigning champ. "How low can you go?"

CONCLUSION

We have been your guide through the transformative journey of fatherhood, from the moment you found out about your child's arrival to navigating the challenges and joys of the first year of parenthood! Here are the key takeaways so you don't forget:

- Fatherhood starts way before the delivery room. Your journey began the moment you found out you were going to be a dad.
- Be there for your partner, especially during pregnancy and childbirth. Your support and presence matter big time.
- Embrace the chaos and cuteness of the first year with all the love and patience you can muster.
- Those tiny milestones? They're the real treasures. Nurture your child's growth and savor every moment with your family.

As we conclude, let's take a moment to reflect on the incredible growth you've experienced since the day you decided to embrace this path. This book has guided you from before your child's birth to the first steps your baby takes in the world. The chapters have delved into each stage, providing insights, guidance, and practical advice to help you navigate the challenges, cherish the milestones, and celebrate the joys of being a dad.

From understanding the physical and emotional changes that your partner goes through during pregnancy to providing unwavering support during labor and delivery, you've embraced your role as a caregiver and nurturer in the first year of your child's life.

The journey has taken you through the trials and triumphs of infancy, from the first smiles and coos to the initial steps and words. You've created lasting memories with your growing baby, capturing each achievement and finding joy in every step. Throughout it all, you've recognized the importance of nurturing your relationship with your partner and forming bonds with your child that will last a lifetime.

As you move forward, remember that fatherhood is a lifelong adventure filled with love, learning, and laughter. Your role as a father is one of continuous growth and transformation, and each day is an opportunity to shape the future of your child's life. Embrace the path ahead with confidence, knowing that you have the knowledge, love, and commitment to be the best dad you can be.

Don't just read about it—embrace each new day, grow with your child, and support your fellow dads. Lastly, if this book has been a source of guidance and support on your journey into fatherhood, consider sharing it with others or leaving a public review of the book. Your review has the power to assist others in finding the invaluable support and insights they require on their own path to fatherhood.

As you close this book and embark on the next chapter of your incredible journey, remember that being a dad is an ever-evolving and rewarding role. Cherish every moment, celebrate every milestone, and keep being the loving and dedicated father that your child is fortunate to have. Congratulations, Dad, on graduating from Daddy Boot Camp and stepping into a future filled with boundless adventures and treasured memories.

REFERENCES

6-Month-Old Baby: Milestones, Weight and Feeding. (2019, August 15). Pampers. https://www.pampers.ca/en-ca/baby/development/article/6-month-old-baby

7 engaging activities for newborns. (2022, April 11). Lovevery. https://lovevery.com/community/blog/child-development/7-engaging-activities-for-newborns/

7 Tips on How to Support Your Pregnant Wife. (2022, October 17). Hello Postpartum. https://hellopostpartum.com/how-to-support-your-pregnant-wife/

20 Week Ultrasound (Anatomy Scan): What to Expect. (n.d.). Cleveland Clinic. https://my.clevelandclinic.org/health/diagnostics/22644-20-week-ultrasound

Allen, N. (2022, May 27). *21 Ways To Prepare For Fatherhood, From The Practical To The Emotional.* Mindbodygreen. https://www.mindbodygreen.com/articles/preparing-for-fatherhood

Attygalla, T. (2022, April 5). *How to set up baby's nursery + nursery set up checklist - nursery design studio.* Nursery Design Studio. https://www.nurserydesignstudio.com/2022/04/05/how-to-set-up-babys-nursery-nursery-set-up-checklist/

Baby Development Month By Month. (2019, November 16). American Pregnancy Association. https://americanpregnancy.org/healthy-pregnancy/week-by-week/baby-development-month-by-month/

Becoming Dad - A guide for new fathers . (2021). Mental Health Foundation. https://www.mentalhealth.org.uk/sites/default/files/2022-06/MHF-Becoming-Dad-A-guide-for-new-fathers.pdf

Benedictus, L. (n.d.). *Fatherhood Can Steal Your Identity: Here's How To Get It Back.* The Father Hood. Retrieved November 7, 2023, from https://www.the-father-hood.com/article/fatherhood-can-steal-your-identity-heres-how-to-get-it-back/

Boyd-Barrett, C. (2021, September 27). Fetal development: Your baby's hearing. *BabyCenter.* https://www.babycenter.com/pregnancy/your-baby/fetal-development-your-babys-hearing_20004866

Bykofsky, M. (2023, June 27). *Babyproofing Your House: A Checklist for Every*

Room. Parents. https://www.parents.com/baby/safety/babyproofing/babyproofing-your-home-from-top-to-bottom/

Cassell, A. (2021). *A childbirth cheat sheet for dads-to-be.* BabyCenter. https://www.babycenter.com/pregnancy/relationships/a-childbirth-cheat-sheet-for-dads-to-be_8244

Common Health Problems and Diseases in Babies. (2021, June 25). Pediatrix. https://pediatrixmd.com/blog/common-health-problems-and-diseases-in-babies/

Corner, N., & Chan, E. (2018, June 17). *What ALL parents should know about parenting.* Mail Online. https://www.dailymail.co.uk/femail/article-5853077/Psychologist-reveals-fathers-guide-bonding-newborn.html

Dad Tribes: Which Type Of Father Are You? (2020). Mr. Porter. https://www.mrporter.com/en-us/journal/lifestyle/dad-tribes-which-type-of-father-are-you-1290010

de Bellefonds, C. (2021, May 14). *What Baby Tastes.* What to Expect. https://www.whattoexpect.com/pregnancy/fetal-development/fetal-taste/

DeMauro, L. (2013, October 15). *The Ultimate Baby Food Allergies Survival Guide.* Precious Little Sleep. https://www.preciouslittlesleep.com/baby-food-allergies-survival-guide/

Development of attachment. (2023, April 25). AboutKidsHealth. https://www.aboutkidshealth.ca/article?contentid=503&language=english#:

Dumaplin, C. (2023a, October 3). *1 Month Old Sleep Schedule.* Taking Cara Babies. https://takingcarababies.com/1-month-old-sleep-schedule?gclid=

Dumaplin, C. (2023b, October 3). *6 Month Old Sleep Schedule.* Taking Cara Babies. https://takingcarababies.com/6-month-old-sleep-schedule?gad_source=1&gclid=

Embracing Modern Fatherhood. (n.d.). Mommy Matters. https://mommymatters.com/blogs/the-motherlode/embracing-modern-fatherhood

Garzón, I. (2021, September 16). *Dad's Role During the Pregnancy.* BellyBelly. https://www.bellybelly.com.au/pregnancy/dads-role-during-the-pregnancy/

James, F. (2022, February 2). *Supporting high-quality interactions in early years.* Education Endowment Foundation. https://educationendowmentfoundation.org.uk/news/eef-blog-supporting-high-quality-interactions-in-early-years

Johnson, N. (2023, October 26). *Baby & Toddler Sleep Schedules With Feedings By Age For Breastfeeding and Formula-Fed Babies.* The Baby Sleep Site - Baby /

Toddler Sleep Consultants. https://www.babysleepsite.com/baby-sleep-feeding-schedules/

Kim, K. (2021, November 5). *Cutest Ways to Document Baby's First Year*. Baby Chick. https://www.baby-chick.com/cutest-ways-to-document-babys-first-year/

Learning your baby's cues. (n.d.). March of Dimes. https://www.marchofdimes.org/find-support/topics/neonatal-intensive-care-unit-nicu/learning-your-babys-cues#:

Lindberg, S. (n.d.). *The couples' guide to sex & intimacy during pregnancy*. Ovia Health. Retrieved October 31, 2023, from https://www.oviahealth.com/guide/103460/pregnancy-sex-intimacy-during-and-after/

Machin, A. (2021, June 19). *In praise of fathers: the making of the modern dad*. The Guardian. https://www.theguardian.com/lifeandstyle/2021/jun/19/in-praise-of-fathers-the-making-of-the-modern-dad

Masters, M. (2021, July 28). *Is Your Baby Going Through a Growth Spurt? Here's How to Tell*. What to Expect. https://www.whattoexpect.com/first-year/ask-heidi/baby-growth-spurts.aspx

McGinn, A. (2019, March 12). *Six Sleep Tips For New Dads*. Good Night Sleep Site. https://goodnightsleepsite.com/2019/03/12/sleep-tips-for-new-dads/

McKay, B. (2013, December 11). *New Dad Survival Guide: The Skillset*. The Art of Manliness. https://www.artofmanliness.com/people/fatherhood/new-dad-survival-guide-the-skillset/

McMaster, H. (2019, March 5). *11 Creative Ways to Document Your Baby's First Year*. Very Anxious Mommy. https://www.veryanxiousmommy.com/11-creative-ways-to-document-your-babys-first-year/

Mindfulness practice with babies. (2021, May 25). Blossom & Berry. https://www.blossomandberry.com/mindfulness-with-babies/

Novak, S. (2020, December 10). *13 Tips for Balancing Work and a New Baby*. What to Expect. https://www.whattoexpect.com/first-year/baby-care/balancing-work-and-new-baby/

Prior, E. (2020, October 12). *10 ways to be an (emotionally) supportive husband during pregnancy*. Professional-Counselling.com. https://www.professional-counselling.com/how-to-be-a-supportive-husband-during-pregnancy.html

Reading Books to Babies (for Parents). (n.d.). Nemours KidsHealth. https://kidshealth.org/en/parents/reading-babies.html

Robinson, L. (2019). *Building a Secure Attachment Bond with Your Baby*. Help-Guide.org. https://www.helpguide.org/articles/parenting-family/building-a-secure-attachment-bond-with-your-baby.htm

Second Trimester- Baby's growth and changes in You. (2023, July 25). Millennium Hospital. https://millenniumhospital.ae/second-trimester/

Sillers, J. (2021, July 25). *Pregnancy Money Moves: Financial Steps for Expecting and New Parents*. MoneyGeek.com. https://www.moneygeek.com/family/resources/financially-preparing-for-a-baby/

Souders, B. (2019, July 4). *Parenting Children with Positive Reinforcement (Examples + Charts)*. PositivePsychology.com. https://positivepsychology.com/parenting-positive-reinforcement/

Steen, M. (2022, September 1). *Why is newborn baby skin-to-skin contact with dads and non-birthing parents important? Here's what the science says*. The Conversation. https://theconversation.com/why-is-newborn-baby-skin-to-skin-contact-with-dads-and-non-birthing-parents-important-heres-what-the-science-says-188927#:

Tanguay, C. (2018, June 27). *Music in Early Childhood: Physical and Cognitive Benefits*. ModulationsTherapies. https://www.modulationstherapies.com/post/music-in-early-childhood-physical-and-cognitive-benefits

Taylor, M. (2021, September 13). *How to Encourage Pretend Play in Babies and Toddlers*. What to Expect. https://www.whattoexpect.com/first-year/play-and-activities/pretend-imaginative-play-babies-toddlers

Taylor, N. (2022, February 28). *Tips for new dads: 33 tips that are great advice for expectant fathers and first time dads*. Fathercraft. https://fathercraft.com/new-dad-tips/

The Best First Foods for Babies 6 to 9 Months. (n.d.). Happiest Baby. https://www.happiestbaby.com/blogs/baby/best-baby-foods-6-to-9-months

The New Dad's Survival Guide: 101 Tips For Dads, By Dads. (2018, March 9). DaddiLife. https://www.daddilife.com/family/expecting/first-time-dads/

Thinking and play: babies. (2018, May 23). Raising Children Network. https://raisingchildren.net.au/babies/play-learning/play-baby-development/thinking-play-babies

Thistel, J. (2022, July 19). *My Sweet Sleeper - Three tips for starting a naptime routine*. My Sweet Sleeper. https://www.mysweetsleeper.com/newborninfantblog/three-tips-for-starting-a-naptime-routine

Toys and materials that support cognitive development. (2020). The University of

Texas Health Science Center at Houston. https://cliengage.org/clirep/ LearnwithMe_ToysMaterialsthatSupportCogDev_2020_09.pdf

Understanding Your Baby's Cues. (n.d.). Texas WIC. https://texaswic.org/health-nutrition/baby/understanding-your-babys-cues

Well-Baby Care Visits & Developmental Milestones (Age 0-12m). (n.d.). Cleveland Clinic. https://my.clevelandclinic.org/health/articles/22063-baby-development-milestones-safety

Wolf, J. (2021, October 25). *10 tips to improve your work-life balance.* BetterUp. https://www.betterup.com/blog/work-life-balance

Made in the USA
Middletown, DE
26 March 2025

73300969R00115